Harrier Carriers

Volume One
HMS INVINCIBLE

Neil McCart

FOREWORD BY REAR-ADMIRAL R. A. G. CLARE

To the memory of the late Admiral Sir Michael Livesay KCB
and all ex-*Invincibles* who have 'Crossed the Bar' in peace and in war.

Cover Design by Louise McCart
© Neil McCart/FAN PUBLICATIONS 2004
ISBN: 1 901225 08 9

Typesetting By: Highlight Type Bureau Ltd,
Clifton House, 2 Clifton Villas, Bradford,
West Yorkshire BD8 7BY

Printing By: The Amadeus Press, Ezra House,
West 26 Business Park, Cleckheaton,
West Yorkshire BD19 4TQ

Published By FAN PUBLICATIONS
17 Wymans Lane, Cheltenham, GL51 9QA, England.
Fax & Tel: 01242 580290
Email: info@fan-publications.i12.com

A magnificent aerial view of *Invincible* at sea showing her flight deck in its final configuration with the forecastle completely plated in.

(Derek Fox)

Contents

Foreword
by Rear-Admiral R. A. G. Clare

HMS *Invincible* exemplifies and justifies the case for Britain to maintain balanced, capable military forces with the flexibility to accommodate unforeseen risks. Conceived at the height of the Cold War against the Soviet Union, she served with distinction in the operations to recover the Falkland Islands and has made a fundamental contribution to coalition operations in every theatre since the fall of the Berlin Wall. Each of these episodes was unheralded and has called for distinctly different capabilities: from anti-submarine warfare in deep water, through air offence and defence in the South Atlantic, to force projection in the littoral. *Invincible* has been there, done that and has several T-shirts to prove it.

This book charts the story of a ship that defined the capability of the Royal Navy in the latter half of the 20th century. Neil McCart has assembled a great deal of detailed material and his account is an excellent summary of the service career of one of Britain's most important warships. Those who served in the ship will find the framework in this book an effective jog for their memories. Those who did not may conjure up their own excitement. Whatever it is that readers imagine to have happened, it was probably worse at the time. For example, Chapter 6 tells us that in 1996, after visiting Izmir (where I assumed command from Captain Ian Forbes), *Invincible* passed south through the Suez Canal; that she visited Dubai, Kuwait and Al Jubail; that it was hot in the Gulf and that the homecoming in Portsmouth was 'just in time for Christmas'. Factually, this brief account is correct, but the three months between Turkey and the UK were filled with intense activity at an exhausting operational tempo, amid substantial uncertainty as to the intentions of the Iraqi regime under Saddam Hussein.

Our preoccupations focused on such questions as: Would we be home for Christmas? Would there be another attack on Western interests in the Gulf? Were we ready to deal with the ensuing military risks? Were there new mines in the northern Gulf? Would the RFA stock Christmas trees? What was it like to sleep for eight hours at a stretch? (On the last one, some thought it best to ask a Wafu). *Invincible* had become the first British carrier to operate in the Gulf in more than 40 years; her visit to Al Jubail was the first ever by an aircraft carrier to a Saudi port. On entry, she flew the flag of Rear-Admiral Alan West, then Commander UK Task Group. We berthed amid much ceremony and carried out a series of official calls. The activities and presence of the *Invincible* task group were widely reported throughout the region and our every move was of great diplomatic significance to deterrence.

Throughout this period, the ship's company performed magnificently. Long periods at high alert were interspersed by short bouts of easier routines in which to recover. Port visits in the Gulf area were enjoyable, but only in Dubai was the local culture sufficiently familiar to Western tastes to enable people to feel at all relaxed. During spells outside the Gulf itself, to the south of the Straits of Hormuz, the flight deck could revert to a sports pitch from time to time and the occasional bar-b-q was a popular way for all ranks and rates to mix. On such evenings it was customary for beer to be sold and for the ship's various musicians to provide entertainment. The bond of mutual trust and respect was such that, despite the sometimes energetic antics of individuals, not a single disciplinary offence came before me as a result of a flight deck banyan. Indeed, it was a tribute to the men and women who served under my command that *Invincible* did everything asked of her, often beyond the limits of reasonable demands. We were never late for a mission; we completed our tasks as ordered and to a high standard.

In an action-packed 1997, we completed a JMC off the North West coast of Scotland on one engine (fuelling over the bow, for safety); held a moving commemoration service in the Bay of Biscay for Diana, Princess of Wales (attended by "more ship's company than come to a clear lower deck", according to the Master at Arms); berthed in Barbados without tugs (the tug skipper was concerned about the flare of the bow, so we put down an anchor and lowered the ship onto the jetty instead); sailed early from Jacksonville (Saddam, again); crossed the Atlantic in five days at an average speed of nearly 30 knots (without breakdown); recovered alive two downed Harrier pilots. In an unprecedented operation at night, involving a high order of seamanship and teamwork, one of the ditched Harriers - an RAF GR7 - was recovered with barely a dent. Two days later, the inverted aircraft was conspicuously visible on deck under a pink and crimson tarpaulin as we entered Barcelona. 'Why make it so prominent, Buffer?' I demanded. 'Barcelona FC colours, Sir!' he replied. I was dubious, but he was right; our aviation embarrassment turned to advantage as we gained positive publicity for our gesture towards the local football heroes.

As usual, the wit and humour of sailors had won through. *Invincible* has had the good fortune to see many comics in her various commissions. I hope that she will see many more and continue to act in the spirit of her namesake predecessors since 1744, and with pride in the traditions of the Royal Navy.

Roy Clare
Rear-Admiral
Director National Maritime Museum, Greenwich
July 2004

Chapter One

The 'Through-Deck Cruiser'
February 1966 – March 1979

'End of fixed-wing flying in the Fleet Air Arm' ...'End of Navy as a Global Force' roared the headlines of daily newspapers on Wednesday 23 February 1966, when the Government of the day cancelled the Navy's proposed new aircraft carrier CVA01, or HMS *Queen Elizabeth* as she was to have been known, and declared its intention of phasing out the Royal Navy's four existing aircraft carriers. At the time it appeared that the political opponents of the Navy's aircraft carrier force had triumphed and that the headlines would prove to be right.

Following hard on the heels of the decision to cancel CVA01 came the Government's announcement of a British withdrawal from bases east of Suez which, although demoralizing to the Armed Services, was an inevitable result of the post-war withdrawal from Empire as most countries of the Commonwealth gained their independence. In place of the Fleet Air Arm's carrier-borne capability, the Government White Paper laid out plans for the role to be: '...more cheaply performed in other ways. Our plan is that in future aircraft operating from land bases should take over the strike reconnaissance and air defence functions of the carrier on the reduced scale which we envisage that our commitments will require after the mid-1970s.'

Without doubt the decisions were a severe blow to the Royal Navy and the sense of crisis was heightened when the First Sea Lord tendered his resignation over the issues involved. However, his successor Admiral Sir Varyl Begg immediately initiated a 'Future Fleet Working Party' under the leadership of Rear-Admiral John Adams, to plan the size and shape of a fleet without aircraft carriers as its main striking force, and it is said they were forbidden to even mention them. The working party quickly came to the conclusion that 'through-deck cruisers', which had originally been envisaged eight years earlier to accompany the fleet carriers on anti-submarine duties, should be considered. Initially the idea was rejected for the political climate of the day was such that aircraft carriers, large or small, were not

As construction of the island superstructure gets under way, *Invincible* takes shape on the stocks at Barrow-in-Furness.
(Mike Smith, BAE SYSTEMS, Marine)

On a dull and wet day *Invincible* takes to the water for the first time as she is launched by Her Majesty the Queen.
(Mike Smith, BAE SYSTEMS, Marine)

Another view of *Invincible* as she is launched.

going to be resurrected. Fortunately, the idea did not disappear altogether, and in 1967 a 12,500-ton vessel, with a cruiser design which could accommodate six Sea King helicopters, was proposed and, more importantly, Government approval for continued planning was obtained. By 1971, in a more sympathetic political atmosphere, the 'through-deck cruiser' design had been enlarged to 19,500 tons, with a capacity for 17 Sea Kings or a similar number of the new Hawker Siddley V-STOL aircraft. Contemporary drawings show the vessel with an unobstructed flight deck running from just aft of the bow to the stern; with an island superstructure, which included masts and funnels, on the starboard side it was apparent that the 'through-deck cruiser' would be an aircraft carrier in all but name. The Royal Navy would continue to be a world-leader in one form of fixed-wing aviation at sea.

With the trials of the V-STOL aircraft having been carried out successfully from *Eagle* and *Ark Royal,* in early 1972 the Ministry of Defence asked Vickers (Shipbuilding) Ltd of Barrow-in-Furness to finalize all the remaining

preparatory work on the design of the 'through-deck cruiser'. On 17 April 1973, some seven years after the formation of the special working party, the first ship of the class was ordered from Vickers, to be built at their Barrow-in-Furness shipyard; she was the largest warship ordered for the Royal Navy since the end of the Second World War. With work on the first 'through-deck cruiser' under way, the development of the P1127 Short or Vertical Take-Off and Landing fighter, reconnaissance and strike aircraft (which had first been considered in 1971 as a naval aircraft) was well advanced and by 1975 it was decided that squadrons of these versatile combat aircraft would be carried aboard the new 'cruisers'. After all the gloom and despondency of the late 1960s and early 1970s, it seemed that the Fleet Air Arm would indeed continue its tradition of fixed-wing aviation.

On 20 July 1973 the first keel plates for the new 'cruiser' were laid on the main slipway at Barrow-in-Furness, the ceremony being carried out by Vice-Admiral Sir George Raper. Initially it was estimated that the cost of

As *Invincible* is towed to her fitting-out berth three Wessex helicopters of 819 Squadron, each streaming a White Ensign, perform a fly-past over the new ship.

(Brian Hargreaves)

Invincible alongside in Buccleuch Dock, Barrow-in-Furness.

(Brian Hargreaves)

Almost ready for sea. *Invincible* undergoes heeling trials while alongside at Barrow-in-Furness.
(Mike Smith, BAE SYSTEMS, Marine)

the new ship would amount to £62 million, and that she would be launched in the summer of 1975. However, with a shortage of skilled labour at the shipyard it was not long before that timetable was abandoned. By mid-1975 work on the new vessel was some 18 months behind schedule, but one piece of good news for the Navy was that they were to take delivery of 25 seagoing versions of the revolutionary jump jet, the Sea Harrier. With its Rolls Royce Pegasus 104 jet engine, the Sea Harrier was to prove an extremely versatile combat aircraft, although in the 1970s it was not seen as a replacement for the Fleet's dependence upon the RAF for its main air support. Initially the requirements for the new cruiser were that she should command a task force and control the operation of shore-based aircraft; act as

anti-submarine warfare commander of a NATO task group, and operate helicopters for such warfare; deploy Sea Harrier fighters for limited air defence, strike and probe missions; deploy Sea Dart surface to air missiles and undertake surface reconnaissance. However, events in the early 1980s were to show that the RAF would be unable to provide the Navy with any air cover at all in some areas of the world, and the 'through-deck cruiser' and her sisters would soon take on the role of light fleet carriers.

By early 1977 work on the first 'through-deck cruiser' was sufficiently advanced for the announcement to be made that the ship would be launched in early May and, as she was the largest warship to be built for many years, the ceremony was to be carried out by Her Majesty the Queen.

Builder's sea trials took place during May and June 1979, in North Channel and the Firth of Clyde...

Tuesday 3 May 1977 dawned dull and wet in Cumbria, with strong south-westerly winds and outbreaks of heavy rain, but despite the inclement weather the ceremony went ahead as planned and thousands of people waited patiently in the rain to see the Queen name the ship *Invincible,* break a bottle of home-made wine over the bow and send the first of the new class of anti-submarine 'cruisers' down the slipway. *Invincible* entered the water with a roar, and was quickly pulled up by tons of drag chains, after which the tugs manoeuvred her into the fitting-out berth in Buccleuch Dock. It was appropriate that the launch was marked by the fly-past of three of 819 Squadron's Sea King helicopters, each streaming a White Ensign, and they were followed by a Harrier flown by Hawker Siddley's chief test pilot, John Farley. As well as flying over the shipyard he was

able to demonstrate the aircraft's versatility by 'taking a bow', before flying south to his base.

With a full load tonnage of 19,810, an overall length of 677 feet (206.3m) and a beam of 115 feet (35m), *Invincible* is a twin-shaft vessel powered by four TBM3 Olympus gas turbines, which generate 112,000 SHP and give her a speed of 28 knots. She has a fuel capacity of 3,000 tons of diesel oil and at an economical speed of 18 knots she has a range of 5,000 nautical miles. Down below, in a spacious, air-conditioned Machinery Control Room, the Engineers, Artificers and Stokers*, control the mighty engines to the quiet hum of distant machinery; there is no sign of grease, or even oil. In place of what once would have been the huge stainless steel control wheels of the engine room starting platform, officers and men control

It is surprising how old titles linger, for clearly none of the men and women on watch in *Invincible's* MCR have ever wielded a shovel to stoke the fierce heat of a coal furnace, but all of them are highly proficient in the use of the most up-to-date computer equipment.

…In the background is the island of Ailsa Craig.

(Ross Gillett, Royal Australian Navy and Fleet Air Arm Museum)

Another impressive aerial view of *Invincible* at sea on her builder's trials.

(Ross Gillett, Royal Australian Navy)

Invincible is gently manoeuvred out of the locks and into the Walney Channel as she prepares to leave Barrow for the last time, to carry out her acceptance trials.
(Mike Lennon)

Once she has passed safely through the locks *Invincible* heads for the open sea, guided by tugs.
(Mike Lennon)

On 19 March 1980 *Invincible* arrived in Portsmouth Harbour for the first time. *(Mike Lennon)*

Invincible's wardroom ante-room and bar at the after end of No 5 deck. *(PO PHOT Paul Smith, HMS Invincible)*

the ship with small switches and levers which might seem more suited to a space module, and they carefully enter temperature and revolution readings into a computer database with the ubiquitous computer mouse taking the place of pencils and large log books. Below them, however, small working parties, oblivious to the roar of machinery around them, still man the cavernous machinery spaces, which are now devoid of watchkeepers, to carry out the routine drudgery of cleaning and polishing.

As built *Invincible's* defensive armament consisted of a single GWS 30 Sea Dart missile launcher, which could be used against both air and surface threats. The most distinctive feature of *Invincible,* and her sisters, is the 'ski ramp' at the forward end of her flight deck which was the original idea of Lt-Cdr Douglas Taylor RN. In a thesis written at the University of Southampton in 1973, he proposed curving up the forward end of the flight deck so that the Harrier could be launched on an upward trajectory. After consultation with Hawker Siddley and acceptance of both the simplicity and benefits of the concept the Harrier design team immediately developed the idea, with a test ramp being built at RAE Bedford. The first 'ramp' take-off took place on 5 August 1976, and as a result of the success of the trials it was decided to fit *Invincible* with a 47-ton, light steel structure with an angle of seven degrees on the port side of the flight deck. This had the effect of adding 1,500lb of payload to the Sea Harrier, and it also enabled the ship to steam at lower speeds when launching aircraft, resulting in a considerable economy as well as extending the ship's endurance at sea. From a pilot's point of view the ramp also increased safety margins. In the event of an emergency at take-off - should the engine nozzles fail to rotate for example - it was calculated that the aircraft would land in the sea two and a half seconds after leaving a flat deck at 90 knots, with a 20-knot wind over the deck. The estimated time for the pilot to react to such an emergency and successfully eject was two seconds. However, a similar emergency, under the same conditions, from an angled ramp would result in a 'splashdown' in six and a half seconds; it was reckoned that an alert pilot would therefore stand a chance of getting away without a ducking. The 500ft-long by 74ft-wide (152.4m x 22.55m) hangar, which runs almost the full length of the ship, is served by two lifts, both of which are 54ft - 6in (16.6m) by 31ft - 8in (9.6m), and are built to a neat scissors design which was originally planned for the ill-fated CVA01, and which allows for open space on three sides of the platform.

Between decks, her 1,100 officers and men live in compact, but comfortable accommodation which sets new standards for the Navy. With most of the ship's company accommodation situated on No 6 deck, gone are the days when mess decks formed part of a main passageway and junior rates, who live approximately 20 to a mess, have comfortable bunks with curtains for privacy, a separate recreation space and an adjoining wash/shower room; all the living accommodation is designated as a 'No Smoking' area. Most junior rates are accommodated forward, with CPOs and POs living in cabins of six with spacious recreation spaces which are very similar in appearance to the wardroom, and senior warrant officers have cabins further aft. Both junior and senior rates' dining rooms are on No 5 deck and right aft on this deck is the wardroom mess, with its dining room and ante-room. Right aft on the decks above are the officers' cabins which are compact and self-contained, as is the suite containing the Admiral's and Commanding Officer's quarters.

In March 1979 it was announced in Parliament that *Invincible,* which had now been redesignated as an 'anti-submarine cruiser', was almost ready to undergo her builder's trials and on Tuesday 20 March the vessel's first commanding officer, Captain Michael H. Livesay RN, who had joined the Navy in 1952 and had served in the destroyer *Aisne* and the aircraft carrier *Hermes* as well as having commanded the minehunter *Hubberston* and the frigate *Plymouth,* took up his appointment in *Invincible.* On Monday 26 March, flying the Red Ensign, *Invincible* left Barrow-in-Furness for dry docking at Greenock and her initial sea trials. These took place off Scotland's west coast, and it was during this period that the first deck landing took place when, with the ship anchored off Largs, a Sea King helicopter of 819 Squadron landed on the flight deck. On board were the First Sea Lord and a US Navy Admiral, who was on a seven-day visit to the UK; it is said he was greatly impressed by what he saw. Upon the successful completion of her trials *Invincible* returned to Barrow-in-Furness for final tests and for her fitting out to be completed in time for her commissioning in early 1980. The original cost of building the ship had risen dramatically, however, and at £215 million she was the most expensive ship ever built for the Royal Navy.

In November 1979, at a Fleet Air Arm dinner, the Prince of Wales, who was the guest speaker, referred to *Invincible* as an aircraft carrier, which was the signal for the various euphemisms that had been used to describe the ship to be dropped. Thereafter she was known as an aircraft carrier, and she was allocated the pennant number R05 which had once been worn by the fleet carrier HMS *Eagle.* On Saturday 15 March 1980, the skyline of Barrow-in-Furness changed perceptibly when *Invincible* made her final departure from Vickers' shipyard to carry out her acceptance trials and to make the passage south to Portsmouth. For the town of Barrow-in-Furness the departure of a newly built ship is always a special occasion, and thousands of people braved a bitterly cold morning to watch *Invincible* as she was nudged through the locks and into the Walney Channel. Four days later, on 19 March, she arrived in Portsmouth Harbour for the first time and

A single-berth cabin for a Head of Department, situated aft on No 7 deck.

(Ross Gillett, Royal Australian Navy)

A senior rates' recreation space and bar.

(Ross Gillett, Royal Australian Navy)

A junior rates' recreation space attached to one of the mess decks.

(PO PHOT Paul Smith, HMS Invincible)

Invincible's main galley. At sea hot meals are provided around the clock.

(PO PHOT Paul Smith, HMS Invincible)

A junior rates' dining hall and serving hatch.

(PO PHOT Paul Smith, HMS Invincible)

secured alongside South Railway Jetty in her base port. That afternoon there was a ceremony in the spotlessly clean hangar, where the ship's company, shipbuilding representatives and the media gathered to witness Captain Livesay sign for the ship and read out a signal from the First Sea Lord, Admiral Sir Henry Leach, who drew attention to the 'Proud day for the Royal Navy, which starts a new era in naval aviation'. He went on to offer:

'Congratulations to you all on bringing into service our first big ship for a quarter of a century.' *Invincible,* the first 'Harrier Carrier', had joined the fleet, but there would be battles ahead, not least those for survival against the cost-cutting Treasury in Whitehall who were always looking out for ways to reduce expenditure, and politicians who were quite willing to sacrifice the nation's defence capabilities for short-term expediency.

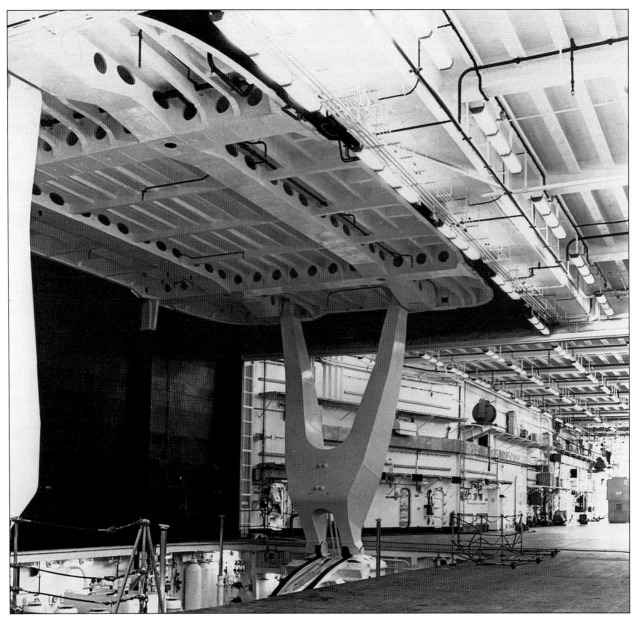

Invincible's hangar and forward lift well. The neat scissors design of the aircraft lifts was originally planned for the ill-fated CVA 01; it allows for open space on three sides of the platform. *(Fleet Air Arm Museum)*

Chapter Two

Commissioning and Preparing for War
April 1980 – April 1982

The first weeks spent in Portsmouth Dockyard were busy ones for both the ship's company and the shore staff as numerous minor fitting-out tasks were completed. The biggest job involved the fitting of two new 18½-ton propellers, which it was hoped would eliminate excessive vibration that had been encountered during full-power trials. The new propellers were more finely balanced and tuned to the performance of the ship's four gas-turbine engines, with the originals being retained in the dockyard as spares. When *Invincible* did put to sea her early sea trials were undertaken in the Channel exercise areas off the Isle of Wight, where all the machinery and equipment was put through its paces. On 2 May she made her first visit to Plymouth and the naval base at Devonport where, in the Hamoaze, she passed the old fleet carrier *Ark Royal* which was laid up and awaiting her final trip to the shipbreaker's yard. Later that month, on 20 May, the first Sea Harrier landed on her flight deck. The aircraft, which belonged to 800 Squadron based at RNAS Yeovilton and piloted by Lt-Cdr Robin Kent, landed on and then left the ship by vertical take-off. He was quickly followed by Lt-Cdr Nigel Ward, the commanding officer of 899 Squadron, who touched down before immediately lifting off again. The carrier's ski-ramp was not to be used until the autumn of 1980 when the ship carried out her 'first-of-class' trials. *Invincible's* initial sea trials continued into June, then in early July, at Portsmouth, preparations began for the commissioning ceremony.

HMS *Invincible* was to have the honour of being the first unit whose commissioning was attended by Her Majesty the Queen, and it took place in the ship's hangar on Friday 11 July. Also present on that fine summer's day were 1,800 members of the ship's company, their families and a number of special guests, including the 85-year-old ex-Royal Marine, William Gasson, the only man still alive from the six who survived the destruction of the battlecruiser *Invincible* at Jutland. After being welcomed to the dockyard by the Flag Officer Portsmouth, the Queen and Duke of Edinburgh were escorted aboard *Invincible* by Captain Livesay. The ceremony began with an interdenominational service conducted by the Chaplain of the Fleet, after which Captain Livesay read the Commissioning Warrant and champagne was served to the guests and ship's company. The commissioning cake, which was a very impressive 1/200th scale model of the ship, designed with the help of builder's drawings and using 37lb of sugar and 28lb of marzipan, was cut by Mrs Livesay, ably assisted by JMEM Michael Davis, the youngest member of the ship's company. During her tour of the ship the

During her extensive period of trials, *Invincible* enters Portsmouth Harbour on 25 May 1980.
(Mike Lennon)

The first Sea Harrier ski-jump launch from *Invincible's* flight deck took place on 30 October 1980. The aircraft, XZ 439, was launched at 10.00 and it was flown by Lt-Cdr David Poole RN.

(Ross Gillett, Royal Australian Navy)

Another view of XZ 439 as it leaves *Invincible's* ski jump for the first such launch at sea. *(Fleet Air Arm Museum)*

Queen saw the main galley, a junior rates' mess deck, the operations room and the flight deck - complete with two Sea Harriers and a Sea King helicopter. From the flight deck the royal party went down to the hangar where they met sailors from all departments of the ship, and their families. Before leaving the carrier that afternoon, the Queen and Duke lunched with Captain Livesay and the ship's officers in the wardroom. HMS *Invincible* was now part of the fleet and the future of fixed-wing flying in the Fleet Air Arm appeared to be secure for many years ahead.

Invincible's trials and work-up, for which she was joined by the Sea Harriers of 800 Squadron, began in the late summer of 1980 in northern waters. Noise-ranging and heeling trials took place in Loch Goil in the Clyde area, and after weapons ranging she made her first foreign visit in the form of a two-day stopover at Stavanger. Prewetting trials were carried out in the North Sea before *Invincible* made a four-day visit to the French naval base at Brest. On 3 October she left home waters for Gibraltar, where she

carried out self-maintenance and the first engine change was performed on a Sea Harrier. During the initial trials period, although Sea Harriers had operated from *Invincible's* flight deck, they had taken off vertically rather than from the ski-ramp. Upon leaving Gibraltar, however, *Invincible* steamed north to the Western Approaches to carry out 'first-of-class' flying trials. For six weeks the Sea Harriers of 800 Squadron, together with Sea King helicopters, carried out launchings and landings in all weathers, day and night. The first launch of a Sea Harrier from the carrier's ramp was undertaken by Lt-Cdr David Poole, flying an aircraft from the experimental establishment at Boscombe Down. During the first week of December there was a setback when one of 800 Squadron's Sea Harriers crashed into the sea about 30 miles off the Cornish coast. Fortunately, the pilot ejected safely and he was quickly rescued by a helicopter, but only small pieces of aircraft wreckage were recovered. With aircraft being launched from the ramp in winds of up to Force 9, the ski-

The first Sea Harrier landing by aircraft XZ 454.

(Fleet Air Arm Museum)

A busy flight deck scene during 'first of class' flying trials. No 60 Sea King is a trials aircraft from Boscombe Down; No 33 is from 824 (C) Flight; No 67 is from 814 Squadron and the Sea Harrier is from 800 Squadron.

(Fleet Air Arm Museum)

ramp concept proved to be more successful than had been originally predicted and on 5 December, after completing her trials, *Invincible* returned to Portsmouth.

In January 1981, with Christmas and New Year leave periods over, *Invincible* put to sea again, and after embarking the Sea Harriers of 800 Squadron she left home waters for the Mediterranean. The crossing of the Bay of Biscay saw the carrier ploughing through gale force winds and heavy seas which sent huge waves crashing over the flight deck and island superstructure. Once into the Mediterranean, however, conditions changed and in calmer seas joint exercises were carried out with the French fleet, including the aircraft carrier *Clemenceau.* During this deployment the aircraft of 800 Squadron* notched up 1,000 flying hours and in the sickbay, when a rating was taken ill with appendicitis, the first surgical operation at sea was performed. *Invincible* called at the French naval base of Toulon, and on the return passage to Gibraltar the Flag Officer Third Flotilla, Rear-Admiral John Cox, hoisted his flag. Finally, on 30 March, after disembarking the aircraft of 800 Squadron, *Invincible* returned to Portsmouth to give seasonal leave and undergo maintenance.

On 21 May 1981, with *Invincible* at sea again, the Sea Harriers of 801 Squadron were embarked and in the following month the ship began her operational sea training off Portland. As always this was a hectic and arduous period, with everyone under great pressure and closed up for long periods without a break. On one occasion, to add to the difficulties, the carrier almost collided with a dredger, and it was only the prompt action by the bridge watchkeepers which prevented what could have been a serious accident. In the event the dredger's skipper was fined for failing to keep a proper lookout. By 9 June, with her long and complex trials and training period over, and her operational sea training completed, *Invincible* had returned to Portsmouth Harbour as a fully operational unit of the fleet.

During the summer of 1981 the personnel of 801 Squadron notched up several notable 'firsts' when, within a very short space of time, they achieved more than 200 deck landings, of which 100 were carried out in less than a month. Two of the squadron's pilots reached personal 'centuries' for night deck landings, while the squadron's RAF pilot (known on board as the 'tame crab') carried out 50 landings, and two other pilots made 30 night-time landings in a very short time. The ship herself took part in a series of NATO exercises, during which she acquitted herself well, and by early December she had returned to Portsmouth for leave and maintenance. It would not be long, however, before *Invincible's* future was in doubt as, like their predecessors in the 1960s, Government ministers were looking for spending cuts within the various departments.

On 21 January 1982, with *Invincible* back at sea, nine

* 800 Squadron eventually joined HMS *Hermes* when her ramp refit was completed, and after *Invincible's* own squadron, 801, had been formed.

pilots of 820 Squadron, including Sub-Lt HRH Prince Andrew, flew their Sea Kings from RNAS Culdrose to join the ship for exercises which would see the carrier operating in her subsidiary role as an LPH (Landing Platform Helicopter). Back in Whitehall, however, *Invincible's* future as a unit of the Royal Navy was looking increasingly uncertain. In 1980, after a great deal of deliberation, the Australian Commonwealth Government announced that approval had been obtained to purchase a new helicopter carrier for the Royal Australian Navy. The proposed new vessel would have to have the capacity to operate V-STOL aircraft, and initially it was thought that a modified US Navy Iwo Jima-class ship would fit the bill, with a definite order being placed during 1982 for delivery some four or five years later*. In the event, during January 1982 the British Government offered to sell HMS *Invincible* to Australia at what was described at the time as a 'knock-down price'. The decision came as part of deep and wide-ranging defence cuts which had been announced the previous year, and which would have seen the withdrawal from service of 17 ships, including *Hermes, London, Glamorgan, Norfolk,* ten frigates, the ice patrol ship *Endurance* and the fast patrol craft *Tenacity.* Although the Defence Secretary had second thoughts about some of the naval cuts, there appeared to be little hope for *Invincible,* which the Australian Navy planned to rename HMAS *Australia,* with the deal expected to be completed by the end of March. It seemed that hopes for the 'through-deck cruiser', which had been conceived as a second-best alternative when it became clear that no British Government, of whatever shade, would build replacement fleet aircraft carriers, had been dashed.

Although there had been protests from Members of Parliament, *Invincible's* reprieve came from a totally unexpected part of the world, and one which no politician had seriously considered to be a potential trouble spot. There is no doubt that the proposed withdrawal of the resident ice patrol ship HMS *Endurance* signalled a lack of British interest in its South Atlantic possessions to the military Junta which had taken power in Argentina. In late 1981 the Argentine Government was complaining to the United Nations about the lack of progress with sovereignty negotiations which had begun in 1979, and which they maintained Britain was deliberately stalling. On 22 December 1981, General Leopoldo Galtieri had succeeded to the Argentine Presidency, as the head of a government whose power lay with a handful of military officers, at the same time retaining his position as the C-in-C of the Argentine Army, an organization whose numbers consisted mainly of unenthusiastic conscripts. On 27 January 1982, as *Invincible* carried out exercises with the Sea Kings of 820

Squadron in northern waters, the Argentine Government made it clear to the British Ambassador in Buenos Aires that British recognition of Argentine sovereignty over the Falkland Islands ('Malvinas' as they were known in Argentina), South Georgia and the South Sandwich Islands, remained an essential requirement for a solution to the dispute. The note to the Ambassador contained strong diplomatic representations such as, 'Argentina demands solutions without further delay or dilatory arguments'. Unfortunately, despite the fact that the 150th anniversary of British possession of the Falkland Islands was approaching, and the fact that there were strong indications that the Argentine Junta wanted to mark the occasion in a very dramatic way, mainly to distract the population's attention from serious economic problems in the country, the matter was not taken too seriously in Whitehall.

Meanwhile in home waters, during February and early March, *Invincible* was exercising in Arctic and Scottish waters, with 820 Squadron and the men of 40 Commando, Royal Marines. The trials in her role as an LPH involved first a company group and then the whole Commando Group, with its vehicles embarking over a three-day period. Two-thirds of the Commando were accommodated on camp beds in the hangar deck, while others were dispersed either in spare bunks, mess deck recreational spaces or other compartments such as the peaceful church on No 7 deck and the weight training room. Following the Commando Group's embarkation they carried out a reinforcement landing on to the Bovington training area, for which the 'sticks' were called forward from the various bed spaces to meet in the hangar, before being taken up onto the flight deck via the forward aircraft lift to be flown ashore. During this period *Invincible* called at Rosyth, and upon her return to Portsmouth in late March many members of the ship's company left the ship to disperse to their home addresses countrywide for their main leave. With the ship at 47½ hours' notice for sea, the aircraft of 801 Squadron disembarked, and conditions on board were relaxed. For most members of the ship's company, like the nation at large, the Falkland Islands were very distant outposts in the South Atlantic, and the shenanigans of a group of Argentine diplomats and 'scrap metal dealers' did not seem to be matters which would affect them. As if to emphasize the normality of the ship's routine, it was announced that on 20 April, when *Invincible* was at sea off the Isle of Wight, the Queen would pay a visit to see both the ship's company and her son Prince Andrew at work, the latter in his role as a pilot with 820 Squadron. Soon after this came the news that later in 1982 *Invincible* was to lead a group of ships on a deployment to the Mediterranean, Persian Gulf and South-East Asia, which was designed to

---

* In anticipation the ageing HMAS *Melbourne* (ex-HMS *Majestic*), which had been launched in February 1945 and completed for the RAN in 1955, was scheduled for paying off on 30 June 1982.

A Sea Harrier FRS1 lands on *Invincible.*

29

re-establish a pattern of Royal Navy group deployments.

As *Invincible* lay alongside, however, diplomatic efforts were being overshadowed by the activities of a group of 'scrap metal' merchants on the small, isolated and hitherto virtually unknown island of South Georgia in the South Atlantic. At 09.00 on 18 March the Argentine Navy transport ship *Bahia Buen Sucesco* anchored in South Georgia's Leith Harbour, without having obtained permission from the British authorities. Soon after her arrival the crew of some 100 officers and men of the Argentine Navy, together with 42 scrap merchants, began unloading stores and preparing themselves for a long stay. Some of the men were carrying firearms and members of the British Antarctic Survey, who were responsible for law and order, heard shooting. Other Argentine sailors hoisted the blue and white Argentine flag over the derelict whaling station at Leith and, as they did not even have permission to land, it was suspected that they were being used as a front to challenge British authority over the island. In London it was agreed that *Endurance,* with a detachment of Royal Marines embarked, would sail for South Georgia to evict the Argentines. On Monday 22 March, before *Endurance* arrived, the *Bahia Buen Sucesco* sailed out of Leith, leaving behind some naval personnel and the scrap metal workers, and on the same day the Governor of the Falkland Islands telegraphed London with information that the Argentines were deliberately flouting British regulations, and that more illegal landings were likely, possibly on the Falkland Islands themselves. On the following day the matter was raised in the House of Commons and over the next two days diplomatic relations between London and Buenos Aires deteriorated rapidly. By 25 March information had been received in London that Argentine warships were being sent to South Georgia to intercept *Endurance,* and it was also learnt that another Argentine naval supply ship, this time flying the flag of the Argentine Navy's Senior Officer, Antarctic Squadron, which was a clear indication of top-level Government backing, had arrived at Leith and not only were personnel landing illegally on the island, but landing craft and military helicopters were operating from the vessel. In London it was feared that any attempt to resolve the situation militarily would provoke a full-scale invasion by Argentina, and further diplomatic efforts were made to remove the Argentines.

On Saturday 27 March intense naval activity at the Argentine bases of Mar del Plata and Puerto Belgrano was observed, with the embarkation of marines and the sailing of several warships, ostensibly for anti-submarine manoeuvres. Two days later it became clear that five Argentine warships, including a submarine, were heading for South Georgia and that another four warships,

including the aircraft carrier *Veinticinco de Mayo**, were also at sea. With many disturbing reports flooding in to Whitehall the decision was taken to dispatch three of the Royal Navy's nuclear-powered submarines to the area, and consideration was also given to the formation of a larger naval force, should it be required. Events had gone beyond the point of no return, however, and at 23.00 local time on Thursday 1 April 1982, heading a massive invasion force, marines of Argentina's elite Amphibious Commando Company landed on the Falkland Islands. Given the size of the force and despite a spirited firefight in which casualties were inflicted on the invaders, it did not take long to overwhelm the token garrison of 80 Royal Marines (double its usual strength at the time), and by 09.30 on 2 April Argentina was in control of both the Falkland Islands and South Georgia. However, in Britain there was an unprecedented national sense of shock and outrage and the decision was taken to send a large naval task force to the South Atlantic to retake the islands.

It was a simple matter to announce the proposed formation and dispatch of a task force, but assembling the huge armada of warships, troop transports and supply vessels to sail some 8,000 miles to the South Atlantic posed enormous logistical problems for the service. One of the main problems was to be that of air cover, for the Royal Navy's big fleet aircraft carriers *Eagle* and *Ark Royal,* with their formidable strike power and AEW capability, had been scrapped in the 1970s, leaving only *Invincible, Hermes* and, if absolutely necessary, the old commando carrier *Bulwark,* which had been laid up for almost a year. Sadly the RAF's boast of the 1960s that they could provide all Britain's air defences had proved to be hollow, and it was obvious that the Navy was the only service which would be able to provide air cover for the proposed landing force. Aircraft numbers would, however, be limited and any serious damage to, or the loss of, an aircraft carrier would jeopardize the success of the whole operation.

On board *Invincible* at Portsmouth, in the quiet, early hours of Friday 2 April, an urgent signal was received on board ordering that the ship be brought to four hours' notice for sea and shortly afterwards, at 06.00, a general recall from leave was commenced, which meant contacting over 500 members of the ship's company. It was the start of an extremely hectic period, which would continue unabated for some five months. That forenoon a signal was received instructing that a full war outfit of ammunition was to be embarked, as well as enormous quantities of stores and equipment, and the ship was to be prepared for extended operations in the South Atlantic. By early afternoon officers and men were returning to the ship from their homes or from holiday destinations, some of whom, after hearing radio broadcasts that *Invincible* had sailed for

Veinticinco de Mayo was ex-HMS *Venerable.*

Invincible and *Bulwark* in Portsmouth Harbour together during the summer of 1981. *Bulwark's* active career was over and she is being de-stored.
(Neil McCart)

southern waters, were surprised to see the ship still firmly secured alongside her berth. By the end of that day, despite the fact that the ship had been at over 40 hours' notice, the engine room department had managed to carry out basin trials on three of the four Olympus main engines. Next day storing and ammunitioning continued apace, as mountains of supplies which had been deposited on the jetty were loaded on board and by midday the ship was at four hours' notice for sea. That afternoon, in the House of Commons, the Prime Minister Margaret Thatcher announced that: 'HMS *Invincible* will lead a naval task group out of Portsmouth on Monday 5 April', which gave just over 48 hours for preparations to be completed. The deployment was to be code-named 'Operation Corporate' which, in view of the proposed defence cuts by a Government determined to run all public services on business lines, was considered both ironic and appropriate.

As the massive effort to prepare *Invincible* and other units for war steadily progressed, the dockyard became a hive of activity. Hundreds of fascinated spectators watched as a procession of helicopters took off and landed on *Invincible's* decks. The carrier's radar aerials circling incessantly and the steady hum of her generators added to the sense of urgency, as dockyard cranes swung backwards and forwards loading supplies on board. Pipes and bells preceded disembodied electronic voices, as a constant stream of orders was broadcast over the ship's tannoy. Just outside the dockyard gate, on The Hard, long queues formed to board the pleasure craft which were offering trips round the harbour, and at Unicorn Gate a steady procession of heavy lorries and fuel tankers went back and forth, day and night, depositing stores on the dockside. Meanwhile, at Yeovilton and Culdrose, 801 and 820 Squadrons were also recalling personnel from leave, and on 3 April ground parties rejoined *Invincible*. At 09.40 on Sunday 4 April, Portsmouth Harbour resounded to the roar of jet engines as the Sea Harriers of the newly enlarged 801 Squadron landed on board after being delayed by fog and, in order that the numbers of aircraft embarked did not become public knowledge, they were quickly struck down. For passengers on the Gosport Ferry it made for an interesting, but deafening, harbour crossing. No sooner had the aircraft arrived than all the ship's trophies and silverware, apart from one battered toast rack which had been damaged during the

1914 Battle of the Falkland Islands, were landed for safe keeping. In contrast to the clamour of activity on the flight deck, down below in the relative calm and quiet of *Invincible's* quarterdeck, four tiny babies, all children of ship's company members, were baptized by the ship's chaplain, the Rev Bill Nelson. In addition there was a visit from the C-in-C Naval Home Command, Admiral Sir James Eberle, and five journalists joined the ship. In view of the massive quantities of ammunition embarked, assurance was sought from the MoD that the magazine decks could bear the additional weight. At 03.00 on Monday 5 April, after almost 72 hours of non-stop work, the embarkation of ammunition was completed, although the loading of stores continued right up to the point when the brow was removed. The last person to leave the ship before she sailed was the Flag Officer Third Flotilla, who had visited to wish all on board good luck.

Finally, at 10.15 on Monday 5 April, a bright and sunny spring day, with her ship's company manning the flight and weather decks and all other harbour traffic at a standstill, *Invincible* slipped her mooring ropes to steam slowly out of Portsmouth Harbour. On the flight deck three Sea Harriers armed with Sidewinder missiles were ranged, while at the stern four Sea Kings, with their rotor blades strapped back, were parked. What took all on board by surprise were the thousands of people who had turned out at Old Portsmouth, Gosport and Southsea seafront, in an extraordinary display of patriotic fervour. On the dockside there were wives and families of the officers and men aboard *Invincible*, and lining the seafront with them were office staff, factory employees and even dockyard workers who, just three days earlier, had received redundancy notices. As *Invincible* sailed past Fort Blockhouse the crowds on the Round Tower, traditionally the gathering point for relatives to wave their farewells to generations of warships which had sailed from the port, cheered and waved their Union Flags and banners. Minutes later the carrier was steaming past Southsea Common and the Naval War Memorial to the men of the two world wars who had lost their lives in defence of the country and, less than ten minutes later, she was steaming out to Spithead and the Channel. Just 21 months after commissioning *Invincible* was sailing to war.

Chapter Three

War in the South Atlantic
April – September 1982

HMS *Invincible* steamed out of Portsmouth Harbour during the forenoon of Monday 5 April 1982, to the strains of Rod Stewart's hit 'Sailing', and as she headed out to Spithead the flags, cheers and tears were left behind on the shores of Southsea seafront as preparations for war began in earnest. 'Hands to Flying Stations' was piped, and it would be some 75 days before the ship's company was stood down and they could relax once again.

At just before midday the first Sea Harrier was launched and another ten sorties followed, with live bombs being dropped in the exercise areas off the Isle of Wight; inclement weather then prevented any night flying. As *Invincible* set course, last minute stores and additional aircrew were flown on board from Portland and Culdrose, and down below efforts continued to find stowage space for the vast quantities which had already been embarked. Deep down in the machinery spaces, however, trouble loomed as the engineers heard strange noises coming from the astern coupling in the starboard main gearbox and, in view of the circumstances and the fact that the ship's forward speed was not affected, it was decided that the ship's engine room personnel would change the coupling whilst the ship was at sea and under way. Dawn on 6 April saw the ship operating with *Hermes* and RFA *Olmeda* some 80 miles south-west of Land's End, and among the mountains of stores still being flown on by helicopter came the new gearbox coupling. With flying operations hampered by poor weather *Invincible* altered course to the south-west to head for the Bay of Biscay, and during the early hours of 8 April, with the starboard propeller shaft locked and the ship's speed reduced, the engineers began changing the three and a half-ton gearbox coupling. Fortunately, as the carrier sailed steadily southward the weather improved, giving way to clear blue skies and calmer seas.

During the passage south anti-submarine manoeuvres were carried out, and 820 Squadron kept two Sea Kings airborne day and night on surface searches and anti-submarine duties. For the squadrons this was a busy period, with continual round-the-clock exercises, and during 9 April the carrier was overhauled and passed by the frigates *Alacrity* and *Antelope*, both on their way south. By the forenoon of 10 April *Invincible* was west of the Canary Islands and just visible to the south-west was *Hermes*. Next day the afternoon was given over to some very welcome recreation which, in warm sunny weather, could be enjoyed on the flight deck. That day *Invincible* was joined by *Broadsword* and *Yarmouth* and as the group sailed southward and approached the equator the weather got hotter and more humid. During 14 April a Soviet 'Bear' reconnaissance aircraft appeared, but this did not prevent an air defence exercise with aircraft from both *Invincible* and *Hermes* attacking each other's ships. On Thursday 15 April, ten days after leaving Portsmouth, with aircraft maintenance being given priority for the day, the flight deck was free for King Neptune to hold court and to inflict a ducking on all who fell foul of his 'policemen' and 'bears', including any journalists who got in their way. Down below, in swelteringly hot and uncomfortable conditions, the engine room department finally completed the difficult task of changing the starboard gearbox coupling. Over the course of seven days three specially selected teams had worked non-stop to complete the hazardous job, but by 16.00 the starboard propeller shaft could be unlocked and *Invincible's* speed was increased from 15 to 22 knots.

At just after midday on Friday 16 April came the first landfall when Ascension Island hove into sight, and by early evening *Invincible* had joined *Alacrity, Broadsword, Glamorgan, Hermes, Yarmouth* and RFA *Sir Tristram* at an anchorage off the island's south-west coast. *Invincible* remained off Ascension for just two days, but during this time everyone was kept extremely busy with even more stores which were being embarked almost continuously. The air defence teams 'intercepted' and 'repulsed' attacks by aircraft from *Hermes,* and the squadrons undertook a full programme of air intercepts and air combat manoeuvring. On 17 April a signal was received ordering *Invincible* to sail at 07.00 the next day, and during the middle watch work began painting grey all the blacking on masts and funnels. By now even the most sceptical observers, who had pronounced that the ship would not 'get beyond Ascension Island' before a diplomatic solution was found, were beginning to appreciate the seriousness of the situation. Maps which had shown the Falkland Islands as just dots in the South Atlantic Ocean were being replaced by those of a larger scale which showed the islands in more detail.

With her ship's company manning the flight deck, a Sea Harrier on the ski ramp and Sea King helicopters ranged aft, *Invincible* makes an impressive sight as, carried out on a wave of patriotic fervour, she leaves Portsmouth Harbour for the South Atlantic on 5 April 1982.
(Mike Lennon)

A bow view of *Invincible* taken shortly after she left Portsmouth for the South Atlantic.

(Imperial War Museum FKD 536)

During the afternoon of 18 April, having refuelled from RFA *Olmeda,* whilst most units of the Task Force steamed south, *Invincible* returned to Ascension Island for a few more hours in order to embark even more stores and ammunition. By evening, however, she was at sea again and heading south to catch up with the remainder of the group, including *Hermes.* Next day, having rejoined the main body, a constant stream of helicopters operated a shuttle service to and from RFA *Resource* as stores were passed to the auxiliary for onward transmission to other units. During the forenoon of 21 April there came the first contacts with the Argentine Air Force when, at just before midday, one of *Hermes'* Sea Harriers intercepted and drove off a 707 reconnaissance aircraft. In the early hours of the next day another such flight, flying at some 38,000 feet, was driven away from the group. This time the aircraft was persistent and it returned twice, on one occasion passing five miles north of the group, before being driven off. That afternoon the flight deck was opened for recreation before the ship went to Defence Stations for two months, with the flight deck placed out of bounds to non-duty personnel indefinitely. That evening at 21.30, however, the group suffered its first casualties when, in severe weather, one of 846 Squadron's Sea Kings was forced to ditch. *Invincible's* helicopters were able to rescue the pilot, but an aircrewman was lost. Soon afterwards the ship went to Action Stations, and then Defence Stations. Thereafter the rig of the day was No 8 action working dress or overalls, with life jackets and anti-flash gear to be carried at all times.

As *Invincible* and her group sailed steadily southwards the weather got cooler and the sea became more unsettled, with 37-knot winds and 15-foot waves crested with dense streaks of foam becoming an everyday sight, although the colder air temperatures made hovering easier for the Sea Harrier pilots. On 25 April there was a boost for morale when it was learned that South Georgia had been retaken, and at 15.45 *Invincible* rendezvoused with *Arrow, Coventry, Glasgow, Sheffield* and RFA *Plumleaf,* before altering course to the north-east towards units which had been left behind at the scene of the previous day's helicopter crash. Later that day, at just before midnight, the whole force turned southward to head directly for the Falkland Islands. Two days later, with Force 7 winds and 20-foot waves, speed was reduced slightly, and on 28 April the Government announced the introduction of an air exclusion zone around the islands, which was in addition to the maritime exclusion zone which already existed. It had become clear by now that the Argentines were ready to fight to defend their illegal occupation.

At 05.30 on Saturday 1 May, a fine, clear day, *Invincible* entered the Total Exclusion Zone (TEZ) and the carrier assumed the vital task of Air Warfare Co-ordinator for the whole force, which gave her responsibility for the conduct of the air battle. As *Invincible* entered the TEZ, a solitary RAF Vulcan bomber arrived after a 15-hour flight from Ascension Island during which it had been refuelled by Victor tankers; its mission was to drop a number of 1,000lb bombs on Port Stanley airport and this was followed up by the dropping of cluster bombs by Sea Harriers from *Hermes.* That forenoon, in response to a report of enemy aircraft approaching the Task Force the carrier went to Action Stations in earnest for the first time. Later in the day two of *Invincible's* Sea Harriers intercepted three enemy Mentor T34C aircraft which were heading towards *Brilliant,* forcing them to ditch their bombs in the sea and escape by making for cloud cover. No sooner had the Harriers returned to their CAP duties than they were directed towards two Mirage IIIs which were in the area. By flying the Harriers slowly north the enemy aircraft were tempted to close the range, and at 15 miles the Harriers turned sharply to face them. The Mirages fired three missiles which were well short, and turned for home before the Harriers were close enough to engage them. At just after 19.00 another Harrier was directed towards a radar contact to the west, to engage two more enemy Mirages, with Flt-Lt P. C. Barton of 801 Squadron scoring the first British kill of the war when he shot down one of the enemy aircraft. That evening, at 20.45, with three enemy Canberra bombers approaching *Invincible,* two Sea Harriers were directed to intercept them and two enemy aircraft were shot down, with the third jettisoning its bombs into the sea and escaping.

In the early hours of 2 May, to allow submarines a clear run at tracking the Argentine aircraft carrier *Veinticinco de Mayo* and her escorts which were at sea north of the Task Force, *Invincible* steered south-east. Soon afterwards, as a precaution against a dawn strike by enemy carrier-based Skyhawk A4 aircraft, the ship's company went to Action Stations. That evening news came in that the Argentine cruiser *General Belgrano* had been sunk by the submarine *Conqueror,* which was a relief to units of the Task Force for, in conjunction with *Veinticinco de Mayo* and her group to the north, she posed a very real threat to the Royal Navy. As it was the Argentine fleet returned to port and did not venture out again during the course of hostilities. Next day two enemy patrol boats which were inside the Total Exclusion Zone were sunk and during the early hours of 4 May another RAF Vulcan raided Port Stanley airport. That afternoon, however, came the first serious setback when HMS *Sheffield,* which was acting as the forward air defence picket, was hit by an air-launched Exocet missile, killing 20 members of her ship's company. Only the discipline and training of the men kept the death toll from being higher. Despite attempts to save the ship she later sank whilst under tow, and her survivors were taken on board *Hermes* and the RFAs. To add to the setback of *Sheffield,* later that day a Sea Harrier and its pilot from *Hermes* were lost over the enemy airstrip at Goose Green. It had been a

Invincible in company with *Hermes* on a dull and misty day during operations in the South Atlantic.

(Imperial War Museum FKD 477)

depressing day, and in addition to the losses suffered by the Task Force it was apparent that a second air-launched Exocet missile had come close to *Invincible* before ditching harmlessly into the sea. It was a stark reminder of the vulnerability of all the ships of the Task Force, which were operating thousands of miles from their nearest base and with limited air cover.

Thursday 6 May was a day dominated by fog and thick sea mists which reduced visibility, and at dawn three Sea Harriers were launched to provide combat air patrols over the hulk of *Sheffield*. Shortly before midday, two of the aircraft which were some miles apart, descended into low cloud to investigate what was thought to be a radar contact and were never seen or heard from again. It was thought that the two Harriers had collided, with the loss of their pilots, Lt-Cdr John E. Eyton RN and Lt William A. Curtis RN, both of whom were very experienced aviators. Despite an extensive search by the helicopters of 820 Squadron and units of the Task Force, no trace could be found of the two men. During the following days *Invincible's* Sea Harriers drove off more enemy aircraft, thus thwarting a number of

air attacks, and on 9 May her ship's company prepared to attack and capture the Argentine trawler *Narwal* which, despite being warned, had continued to spy on the movements of the Task Force. A boarding party was flown the 150 miles to the trawler which, having been strafed by Sea Harriers, quickly surrendered. The trawler had been commanded by a naval lieutenant commander and investigations revealed military documents showing the vessel had been ordered to keep surveillance on units of the task group. In the event the 24 crew members were taken on board *Invincible*, where they were kept under guard in the chapel on No 7 deck. One of three casualties died from his injuries and on 10 May he was buried at sea. By this time units of the Task Force were carrying out regular bombardments of Argentine positions on the Falkland Islands, and during a night passage through the Falkland Sound *Alacrity* engaged and sank an 830-ton Argentine supply ship, *Isla de los Estados,* off the Swan Islands. During 12 May, despite inclement weather with winds of up to 40 knots, enemy aircraft made two raids on the Task Force during which a bomb hit the destroyer *Glasgow*, but passed

Maintenance teams working on a Sea Harrier during operations off the Falkland Islands.

(Imperial War Museum, FKD 538)

A Sea Harrier two-seat trainer on *Invincible's* flight deck. The markings indicate that the aircraft is one from the BAE factory at Dunsfield which was sent to augment the Task Force.
(Imperial War Museum FKD 597)

complex amphibious assault.' The enemy raids concentrated on the frigates in San Carlos Water, which were providing anti-aircraft cover, and as well as falling victim to the anti-aircraft barrage some Argentine aircraft were shot down by 801 Squadron's Sea Harriers. Although the landings were a success the Argentine air attacks took their toll on the naval units protecting the area, with both *Argonaut* and *Antrim* being hit by bombs which failed to explode, while *Ardent* was lost after being hit by at least ten bombs, which left 22 members of her ship's company dead. So deadly were 801 Squadron's Sea Harriers, however, that it was said that the Argentine pilots referred to the dark-grey painted aircraft as 'El Muerta Negra' or 'The Black Death'.

In the days which followed the landings *Antelope* and *Coventry* were lost to enemy action and at 19.42 on 25 May the vital supply ship *Atlantic Conveyor,* which was only two miles from *Invincible,* was hit and sunk by an Exocet missile. A few minutes after the merchantman was hit a low, fast contact was detected on the radar

right through the ship without exploding and *Invincible's* shipwrights helped to repair the damage.

On 19 May *Invincible's* group rendezvoused with the Amphibious Group led by *Fearless,* and during the morning watch of 21 May, while *Invincible* and her group created diversions to the south of the islands, the main landings took place in the San Carlos area to the north-west of East Falkland Island. By the forenoon of that day Argentinian aircraft, flying from their mainland bases, had begun a series of intensive and sustained bombing raids on the units in San Carlos Water which have been described by one naval officer who was there as, '…a toe-to-toe slugging match, a vicious fight that ensured the ultimate success of a

screens, which was thought to have been an incoming Exocet missile, and three salvoes of Sea Dart missiles were fired in quick succession. Despite the continual Argentine air attacks there is no doubt that *Invincible's* round-the-clock combat air patrols prevented even more damage to units of the Task Force while the loss of this vital aircraft carrier would have had serious consequences for the whole operation. During the afternoon of Saturday 29 May, with winds of up to 27 knots and heavy seas, a Sea Harrier which was about to be launched, pivoted and rolled over the edge of the flight deck. Fortunately, at the very last moment, the pilot, Lt-Cdr C. M. Broadwater, was able to eject into the sea and was rescued safely. The aircraft had

Invincible off the Falkland Islands, 12 June 1982. Ready to launch are two of 801 Squadron's Sea Harriers. The lighter coloured aircraft belonged to 809 Squadron.
(Fleet Air Arm Museum)

The frigate *Andromeda* leads *Bristol, Invincible* and other units of the Task Force.

(Fleet Air Arm Museum)

Invincible anchored at Port William, Falkland Islands, close to where her predecessor had moored in December 1914 before steaming out to engage Admiral Graf Spee's Squadron.

(Imperial War Museum FKD 2598)

been at its take-off position when the ship, which was turning into the wind, rolled heavily, causing the Sea Harrier's nose wheel to castor under its heavy load and slide uncontrollably across the flight deck and into the sea.

Meanwhile, ashore on East Falkland the Army had captured Goose Green, together with 1,200 prisoners, as they prepared for the march on Port Stanley. It was clear that the land campaign was progressing well and on board *Invincible* the Sea Harriers continued their patrols, with the Sea Kings of 820 Squadron acting as the workhorses of the Task Force. In addition to their anti-submarine duties they carried out search and rescue operations, and were constantly ferrying personnel, ammunition, stores and any other commodity which was required urgently. On the Argentine mainland newspapers carried reports of *Invincible's* demise, and one journal even printed a 'photograph' of the carrier with thick black smoke pouring from her. It was said that a copy of the latter found its way into *Invincible's* Damage Control HQ, under which one wag had added the caption, 'Damage Control Saved HMS *Invincible*'.

On 1 June, at the conclusion of a CAP sortie, one of 801 Squadron's pilots, Flt-Lt I. Mortimer, was reported as overdue, and it was presumed that his Sea Harrier had been shot down. Despite the fact that a prompt search and rescue operation was mounted there was no trace of the pilot, although hope was kept alive by an Argentine radio news report which stated that a parachute had been seen descending into the sea. At 02.30 the next morning the pilot was located and rescued by one of 820 Squadron's Sea King helicopters. It transpired that Flt-Lt Mortimer had been keeping observations on aircraft movements at Port Stanley airport when his Harrier was hit by a ground-to-air missile, and he was forced to eject into the sea. Having successfully clambered into his dinghy he had to lie low as on two occasions he was overflown by an Argentine aircraft before, finally, after a nine-hour search, he was rescued. Later on 2 June the Sea Harriers flew continuous patrols to protect the landing of reinforcements that had been brought from South Georgia in the transports *Canberra* and *Norland*. Also that day came the news that Australia's Government was offering to delay or even cancel the proposed purchase of *Invincible*.

On 5 June, with visibility seriously reduced by thick fog, *Invincible's* Sea Harriers continued to fly their patrols, but the hazards of flying in such conditions were highlighted by the experiences of Lt C. Cantan who, upon his return to the ship, was unable to find *Invincible* as she was enveloped in fog. On his first approach he could not see the ship at all and, despite the fact that he was almost out of fuel, he was forced to go round again. Fortunately, to the relief of all, he managed to pick up the carrier and make a good landing, but with only 150lb of fuel remaining it had been a close call. Next day, in response to

an Argentine bombing attack on the troops ashore, *Invincible* and *Brilliant* detached from the main group to within 100 miles of the Falklands' coast in an effort to catch either an enemy Canberra bomber or a Hercules aircraft, but without result. On 8 June came the tragic bombing of the RFAs *Sir Tristram* and *Sir Galahad* at Bluff Cove, although during the next enemy air raid all four Mirage IIIs were shot down by Sea Harriers from *Hermes*. Despite the setback at Bluff Cove the land forces ashore were closing in on Port Stanley and it was only a matter of time before the islands were recaptured.

Wednesday 9 June found *Invincible* operating a good distance from the islands, and most of the day was spent replenishing and stowing stores from RFA *Fort Grange*. For the first time the Sea Harriers were able to use a landing strip ashore for refuelling, which was a major advantage for the aircraft of the Task Force. Next day 820 Squadron landed a detachment at San Carlos to carry out intelligence-gathering duties for Commodore Amphibious Warfare. By Friday 11 June naval units were carrying out an intensive bombardment of the area around Port Stanley, but the Argentines were still fighting back and at just before dawn on 12 June the destroyer *Glamorgan*, which was leaving the gun line after a night bombardment, was hit by an Exocet missile. The missile hit the ship as she was executing a turn and heeling to port, passing through her topsides aft on the port side, and entering the hangar where it set the Wessex helicopter on fire before starting another fire in the galley below; it finally exploded in the Gas Turbine Room. Fortunately, magnificent efforts by the ship's company prevented the fires from getting out of control and she was still able to make 18 knots while Sea Harriers from *Invincible* patrolled overhead to prevent any further attacks on her. As *Glamorgan* came within range of the carrier a doctor was transferred, and five casualties were taken to *Invincible's* sickbay. Sadly, one man was so seriously injured that he died shortly after his arrival on board.

Ashore, meanwhile, the land campaign was in its final stages and during the early hours of 13 June the Army captured key positions around Port Stanley. Twenty-four hours later the final assault began, and Sea Harriers from *Invincible* prevented a number of enemy air attacks on the troops occupying the high ground around Port Stanley. At 18.07 on 14 June, to everyone's relief, a white flag was seen flying over the town and later that evening, in gale force winds and heavy snowstorms, the Senior Pilot of 820 Squadron, who was leading the shore detachment, was ordered to fly to *Fearless*. Once there he was directed to Fitzroy where he picked up Major General Moore and flew him to Stanley to take the surrender of Argentine forces. The surrender was effective from 23.59 that day, and suddenly the priority became the disarming and repatriation of the Argentine Army.

During the forenoon of 28 August 1982 *Illustrious* took over from *Invincible* in the South Atlantic. In this view the two carriers are seen steaming together before *Invincible* left for the long voyage home.

(Fleet Air Arm Museum)

Surrounded by small boats, *Invincible* moves towards her berth in Portsmouth Harbour following her return from the South Atlantic. Here she is being saluted by the US Navy's destroyer *Compte de Grasse*.

(Mike Lennon)

45

The surrender of the Argentine forces had come just in time, for in the South Atlantic it was midwinter with wind speeds of over 40 knots and mountainous seas accompanied by icy-cold snowstorms, so that conditions had deteriorated considerably in the weeks since *Invincible* arrived in the area. At midday on Tuesday 15 June, with the carrier being battered by the high winds and heavy seas, the flight deck handlers were required to move a Sea King which was being damaged by waves and spray. Moving the helicopter was a routine task which was carried out regularly in all weather conditions, and on this occasion it did not prove a difficult problem. However, as the flight deck tractor was about to be secured a sudden lurch of the ship sent it sliding out of control. The vehicle collided with another tractor which had been battened down, breaking the chains and sending it sliding into the island superstructure, where it pinned Naval Airman (AH) B. Marsden against the outer bulkhead. Despite prompt medical attention and a major surgical operation lasting several hours, NA Marsden died from his injuries. This tragic accident cast a shadow over the euphoria of victory and at 13.30 the next day, in a position Lat 51° - 35'S/Long 53° - 48'W, at a service attended by over 200 members of the ship's company, he was buried at sea.

Despite the fact that the war was over and many units were heading north for home, *Invincible* was required to stay in the vicinity of the Falkland Islands until the end of August, although with hostilities over the ship was to be allowed a period of rest and relaxation in warmer waters to the north. During this period and before she left for home, *Hermes* provided the air defence capability for the Falkland Islands. During the period of hostilities 801 Squadron had flown some 599 combat missions for a total of 786 hours. They had dropped 56 bombs, expended 3,061 rounds of 30mm ammunition, as well as 12 Sidewinder missiles, destroying some seven Argentine aircraft, with three more probable victims. The crews of 820 Squadron had been called upon to perform a variety of tasks, from search and rescue, transferring stores and ammunition, rescuing survivors from the sea and from damaged ships as well as delivering mail, all in addition to their anti-submarine duties. In the course of four months the squadron clocked up the equivalent of 18 months of peacetime flying and, thanks to the ground crews, kept up an almost 100 per cent serviceability record.

At 22.24 on Friday 18 June, in company with *Andromeda*, *Invincible* set course north for warmer weather and next day the ship's company fell out from Defence Stations. There also came the heartening news that, three months ahead of schedule, the second Invincible-class aircraft carrier, HMS *Illustrious*, had left Swan Hunter's shipyard on the River Tyne and, having been accepted into the Royal Navy, she would be in the South Atlantic to relieve *Invincible* by the beginning of September. As the carrier made her way towards the tropics the Engine Room Department began the task of changing one of the ship's gas turbine main engines, the first time such an evolution had been attempted at sea. Changing the massive three-ton engine was an extremely delicate and difficult task, and at moments during the operation the ship was steered slowly down sea in order to minimize the pitching and rolling, particularly when the new turbine was manoeuvred into position in the casing. A week after leaving the Falkland Islands *Invincible* was in the vicinity of Latitude 23° when she rendezvoused with the destroyer *Bristol,* the North Sea repair ship *Stena Inspector* and the cable ship *Iris,* all of which had sailed down from Ascension Island to assist with the carrier's self-maintenance. There was also a visit from the Flag Officer Third Flotilla who addressed the ship's company and toured the ship, and deck sport tournaments were held against teams from *Andromeda*. There was also the sight of *Glamorgan* and *Plymouth* as they steamed past on their way home, and a highly successful 'street party' was held on the flight deck, which raised a good sum of money for the South Atlantic Fund which had been set up. Down below the engineers completed their main engine change, and by Thursday 1 July *Invincible* was back in the Total Exclusion Zone, with the ship's company at Defence Stations and flying having begun in earnest once again.

During *Invincible's* second period off the Falkland Islands, some 80 to 150 miles east of Port Stanley, she operated in bitterly cold weather, with frequent heavy snow squalls, blinding snowstorms and very heavy seas. This time, however, there were regular deliveries of both stores and mail. As the carrier provided the air defence capability for the Falkland Islands, more units began their long passage home. Among these was the destroyer *Cardiff* and the elderly, 22-year-old Rothesay-class frigate *Yarmouth*, which had been present at the surrender of the Argentine force on South Thule in the Sandwich Islands. The departure of these two vessels left *Invincible* as the only unit of the original Task Force remaining in the waters of the South Atlantic. During her patrols the Sea Harriers of 801 Squadron flew high-profile surface searches of the seas around the islands in order to remind the Argentines of her presence and on Monday 12 July, for the first time since her departure from Ascension on 18 April, land was sighted in the form of the distant hills of the Falkland Islands, although they were hidden for a time by heavy squalls of rain and sleet. Next day came the news that *Invincible* would definitely not be sold to Australia. On Tuesday 20 July, while carrying out a four-ship replenishment, *Invincible* closed to within five miles of the north-east coast of East Falkland where, in the calmer waters, the air engineers were able to carry out a Harrier engine change. During the days which followed the carrier closed the shore again, this time to operate her aircraft over the islands.

On Wednesday 21 July *Hermes* arrived back in Portsmouth to a tumultuous welcome, but for *Invincible* there were still weeks of patrolling the grey, inhospitable waters of the South Atlantic. During this period the ship's company found a variety of ways to wile away the time and to amuse themselves. Some attended GCE 'O' level classes while others opted for fitness training, mess games, deck sports, chess competitions, an Arts and Crafts Exhibition and even a grand beard-growing contest. All the time, as the days and weeks rolled by, *Invincible* herself patrolled the Falkland Islands Protection Zone, as the TEZ had been redesignated, more often than not in foul weather conditions with gale force winds and enormous seas. On a more upbeat note there was some relief when, on Monday 2 August, it was learned that *Illustrious* had left the UK for the long passage south to relieve her older sister in the South Atlantic. Sunday 15 August saw *Invincible* in Berkeley Sound where a disabled GR3 Harrier was lifted ashore by Chinook helicopter, and after two days back at sea carrying out anti-submarine exercises, on 18 August the carrier anchored in San Carlos Water. Although her stay was limited to just a few hours, the ship's company had an opportunity to see the place from where the amphibious landings had been launched, and where the frigates responsible for the protection of the amphibious force had borne the brunt of the Argentine air assault. Next day the overwhelmingly popular members of 'Operation Showboat' arrived on board, six entertainers who had made the long journey by air and by sea from the UK to entertain the British forces in the South Atlantic. In the words of one member of the ship's company, 'Bobbie Knutt, Roger and Celia Hawkins made us laugh and sing whilst the pretty trio of dancing girls 'Dream', two Carols and Tracey, kept us riveted by their singing and dancing. We paid close attention to the girls since we had been warned that this was to be our only recognition exercise before our return to Portsmouth.' The final curtain call was taken by the six entertainers and the popular Captain J. J. Black, *Invincible's* commanding officer. Two days later, on Saturday 21 August, *Invincible* remained hove to for most of the day as severe gales and mountainous seas swept the area, sending the smaller escort ships inshore for shelter. It was a reminder of what a winter in the South Atlantic could mean.

Tuesday 24 August saw an event of unique historical significance when *Invincible* anchored at Port William, very close to where her predecessor had moored in December 1914 before steaming out to engage Admiral Graf Spee's Squadron, which had wreaked havoc on Admiral Cradock's Squadron at Coronel. Following that first battle of the Falkland Islands the Royal Navy's battle fleet had returned successfully to Port William and a celebratory mess dinner had been held in the battlecruiser *Invincible's* wardroom. Sixty-eight years later a similar celebratory dinner was held

in the aircraft carrier's wardroom. One of the guests was Rex Hunt, the Civil Commissioner and former Governor of the Falkland Islands and another was Vice-Admiral William Staveley, the incoming C-in-C Fleet and the grandson of Vice-Admiral Sir Doveton Sturdee who, flying his flag in HMS *Invincible,* had commanded the Battlecruiser Squadron 68 years earlier. Next forenoon, after the helicopters of 820 Squadron had flown on three Argentine 30mm guns for delivery to museums in the UK, *Invincible* weighed anchor and left a bright and clear outer harbour for the grey waters of the South Atlantic.

At just before dawn on Friday 27 August came the event for which everyone on board *Invincible* had been waiting, when *Illustrious* was sighted by lookout Steward S. Marsden. It too was an event of historical interest for it was the first meeting of the two sister ships. There then followed 36 extremely busy hours during which large quantities of stores were transferred to *Illustrious* before, finally, during the afternoon of 28 August, she made a very impressive steam past to 'much wild and enthusiastic waving and cheering' from '*Invincibles*'. That evening, at 20.00, over the ship's broadcast system, *Invincible's* Navigator gave the order: 'Steer 055. Revolutions 186'. At last, in company with *Bristol*, she was heading for home. That evening, as she sailed steadily north, she received the following signal from the C-in-C Fleet: 'I would like you, your ship's company and your embarked squadrons to know of my personal appreciation and admiration of all your endeavours in the South Atlantic. Every man may take just pride in the fortitude, courage and professionalism that has been *Invincible's* hallmark throughout her time in the Battle Group. I wish you a safe and restful journey north and look forward to your joyful homecoming.'

As *Invincible* sailed north the weather became warmer and the seas bluer. For the ship's company there was a painting and cleaning programme to be completed while for the sun worshippers among them there was an unusually quiet flight deck upon which they could relax. The start of September was marked by the reversion to peacetime cruising and as the ship entered the tropics the ship's company put on a very popular 'sods opera'. On Monday 6 September *Invincible* arrived off Ascension Island where, on shore, 100 runners set a record for a 100 x one mile relay race and where the anglers were able to indulge in their sport. Next day an advance leave party left the ship to be flown home and that afternoon *Invincible* weighed anchor to begin the next leg of her passage north. During the afternoon of 8 September, almost five months since her southbound crossing, the carrier crossed the equator and shortly after this she rendezvoused with HM Ships *Glasgow, Newcastle* and *Phoebe,* as the three units took a short break from their passage to the South Atlantic. With Her Majesty the Queen due to join the ship at Spithead for the ceremonial entry into Portsmouth

Invincible returns in triumph to secure alongside her berth in Portsmouth Dockyard where families and friends wait to greet their loved ones.

(Fleet Air Arm Museum)

Harbour, the cleaning and painting programme continued, and all the time *Invincible* drew closer to her home port.

On Wednesday 15 September, with rehearsals for the entry into Portsmouth taking precedence over the painting, *Invincible* entered the Bay of Biscay. Fortunately, this unpredictable stretch of water was on its best behaviour which allowed the RAF to fly a virtual army of press photographers overhead, which was an indication of the intense national interest in *Invincible's* homecoming. At 08.00 next day, in thick fog, the carrier anchored in Mounts Bay, Falmouth, where members of the press were embarked, and at 16.00 she weighed anchor and with *Bristol,* set course up Channel. During the afternoon the First Sea Lord, Admiral Sir Henry Leach, embarked by helicopter and at 05.30 the following morning hands were called early and the ship anchored in a fog-bound Spithead. That morning and forenoon the ship was a hive of activity, with visits from numerous VIPs and even more press representatives. Without doubt, however, the least popular visitors were from the Customs and Excise for, as one member of the ship's company recalled, 'Where they thought we had been able to get ashore to buy anything mystified us all.'

Meanwhile, at Portsmouth sightseers were lining vantage points all round the harbour and along Southsea seafront, while in the Solent hundreds of small boats, yachts and launches gathered to escort *Invincible* into her home port. At HMS *Vernon**, the Queen, Duke of Edinburgh and Princess Anne boarded a barge which took them out to the aircraft carrier, where they arrived at just after 11.00. After being greeted by Admiral Leach and Captain Black they had a private reunion with Prince Andrew before touring the ship, and meeting members of the ship's company, on their way to the bridge. *Invincible* weighed anchor at 11.45 and as she got under way she was surrounded by hundreds of small craft of every description, including canoes paddled by intrepid youngsters. With fireboats spouting plumes of water, and accompanied by her armada of small craft, which had grown so large that it seemed to fill the whole of Spithead, *Invincible* led *Bristol* and RFA *Olna* through the deep water channel and along a Southsea seafront which was packed with eager sightseers all waiting to catch a glimpse of the carrier as she returned in triumph from the South Atlantic.

On board *Invincible* the ship's company proudly manned the flight and weather decks, while a Royal Marines Band accompanied by 12 pipers of the Scots Guards played the ship in. As she passed the Round Tower, which for hundreds of years has been the traditional point of farewell and greeting for naval ships sailing to and returning from war, there was more banner waving from the enthusiastic crowds. They were accompanied by a cacophony of noise from car horns, ships' sirens and cheering from both sides of the harbour and from ferries, yachts, dinghies and all manner of small craft, manned by both professional sailors and amateurs and, in one case, to the delight of the ship's company, by topless girls. It was an outpouring of the whole nation's gratitude and respect for the achievements of *Invincible* and her company in the South Atlantic.

As she was manoeuvred alongside the dockyard's West Wall there was an equally enthusiastic welcome from families and friends of the ship's company, who released hundreds of red, white and blue balloons. She had spent 166 days at sea, during which she had been a prime target for the Argentine Air Force; she had seen the campaign through from start to finish and, in order to provide the island's air defences until the RAF could operate from Port Stanley, she had remained behind long after all the other units had left. Once the royal party had disembarked the ship's company was able to swarm ashore to greet wives, relatives and friends. *Invincible's* service in the South Atlantic is perhaps best summed up by Admiral Refell when he signalled: 'No other ship has contributed so much to the success of the Task Force Group operations.'

---

* HMS *Vernon* is now Gunwharf Quays, one of Portsmouth's premier shopping and leisure facilities.

Chapter Four

'Orient Express' to the Caribbean
October 1982 – May 1986

The Falklands War had seen *Invincible* at sea for 166 days, which was the longest ever period of continuous carrier operations, during which time she had clocked up 51,660 miles, the equivalent of twice round the world. During this time she manufactured enough fresh water to fill 45 Olympic-size swimming pools and the galley had produced some 38,000 gallons of tea. Apart from the brief period of self-maintenance at sea in the southern Atlantic Ocean, the ship's machinery and equipment had been running continuously, often at sustained periods of full power and a refit was now necessary in order to prepare the carrier for further service. In the event *Invincible's* refit saw her in Portsmouth Dockyard for the remainder of 1982, during which time she was fitted with Vulcan Phalanx C1WS weapons, and the C-in-C Fleet, Admiral Sir William Staveley, raised his flag in the ship.

In mid-January 1983, for the first time since returning home from the Falklands, *Invincible* sailed from Portsmouth to carry out an intensive programme of sea trials. On 13 January, while *Invincible* was exercising with *Hermes* in a stormy Channel, a Sea King helicopter from the carrier went to the aid of the 600-ton Greek cargo ship, MV *Georgios,* which was off Beachy Head and listing badly after her cargo had shifted. The helicopter stood by as six crewmen were taken off by the Newhaven lifeboat and the ship's master and chief engineer took the vessel into the safety of the Sussex port. On 1 February *Invincible* left Portsmouth to take part in NATO exercises in the Atlantic, and in a deployment to the Caribbean, code-named 'Caribtrain 83', for which she embarked the Sea Harriers of 801 Squadron and the Sea King helicopters of 820 Squadron. Escorted by destroyers, including *Battleaxe* and *Bristol,* and frigates which included *Arethusa, Euryalus* and *Zulu,* and also accompanied by the RFAs *Olwen* and *Resource,* she encountered severe gales and heavy seas which disrupted flying operations. Two days after leaving Portsmouth, whilst carrying out deck landing practice off the coast of Portugal, one of 820 Squadron's helicopters crashed into the sea some six miles away from the ship, killing the pilot, Sub-Lt Malcolm Kelham. During her first transatlantic crossing *Invincible* exercised with her escorts and, some 200 miles south of Bermuda, she took *Bristol* in tow. The two-month deployment

included exercises off the Bahamas and Belize, as well as some popular runs ashore in the West Indies. The main exercise off the Bahamas took place on the US Navy's underwater test range near Andros Island, during which HMS *Splendid* took on the role of 'enemy' submarine, and air and surface missiles, including Ikara, were launched. Following this exercise the group split up, with *Battleaxe* and five frigates heading for the eastern Caribbean while *Invincible, Bristol* and the RFAs sailed west to Belize. Sea Harriers from the carrier exercised with land-based RAF GR3 Harriers over the rainforests of Belize, while 820 Squadron took on a troop-carrying role in the more remote parts of the country. The ships were also involved in a series of visits, with *Invincible* calling at Montego Bay, Jamaica and Nassau, before carrying out further weapons training and self-maintenance.

Following her successful Caribbean deployment *Invincible* crossed the Atlantic once again, this time bound for Gibraltar. As she approached the colony there was an unusual air defence exercise as the carrier was overflown by a USAF B52 bomber, which was on a long-distance sortie from its base in New York State. Aircraft from 801 Squadron intercepted the bomber as it approached *Invincible* and made low-level passes over the ship. At Gibraltar, with 15 other surface ships and submarines, she took part in 'Exercise Springtrain', which took her both to the east and west of The Rock. The units led by *Invincible* rotated between the Atlantic and Mediterranean exercise areas so that firings against both air and surface targets could be carried out. Missiles fired included Exocet, Ikara, Sea Dart, Sea Wolf and Seacat. Two hulk targets, one of which was the old paddle tug *Faithful* which had once been a familiar sight in Devonport Dockyard, were sunk by missiles, rockets and even old-fashioned gunnery, as well as bombs from *Invincible's* Sea Harriers and RAF Buccaneers. The Sea Kings of 820 Squadron got some anti-submarine practice against the submarines *Splendid* and *Otus.* The exercises were controlled from *Invincible,* and their aim was to provide advanced training in all spheres of maritime warfare. The internal security exercises took on a little added realism due to the fact that the Spanish Government sent an 'urgent note of protest' and urged its citizens to boycott the colony while the naval exercises were under way. During the evening of Thursday

A very smart *Invincible* leaving Gibraltar on a wet day in April 1983 for 'Exercise Springtrain'.

(*Mike Lennon*)

Another excellent view of *Invincible* with two Sea Harriers and five Sea Kings ranged on the flight deck as she leaves Gibraltar in April 1983.   *(Mike Lennon)*

14 April Sea Kings from *Invincible* were involved in a mercy mission when a distress signal was picked up from the master of a semi-submersible oil rig which was under tow from Bilbao to eastern Spain. Two of 820 Squadron's Sea Kings flew 130 miles in 70-knot winds and poor visibility to rescue the oil rig's master who had suffered back and leg injuries. On the return journey they had to refuel at Tangier, but the injured man was delivered safely to hospital at Gibraltar. At the end of the exercises *Invincible* returned to Portsmouth, where she arrived during the last week of April.

In May 1983, with leave and maintenance complete, *Invincible* took part in 'Exercise High Tide', which involved the ship taking on the LPH role with the Royal Marines of 45 Commando, Dutch Marines and the Sea King helicopters of 845 and 846 Squadrons. After practice assaults on Den Helder and visits to the ship by the Netherlands Defence Minister and MPs from the Dutch Parliament, the marines were flown off the ship for training with 3 Commando Brigade on Salisbury Plain. For *Invincible,* the highlight of 1983 was to be the start of her seven-month deployment East of Suez, leading the 'Orient

Express' task group. With seasonal leave over the deployment began during the first week of September when the carrier rendezvoused with other ships, including the destroyer *Nottingham,* the frigates *Achilles, Aurora* and the elderly *Rothesay,* as well as the submarine *Opossum* and the RFAs *Appleleaf* and *Olmeda.* In command of the task group was Rear-Admiral Jeremy Black who flew his flag in *Invincible* and who, only 12 months before, had been in command of the carrier. Off the coast of Cornwall the ship received a visit from the new Defence Secretary, Michael Heseltine, who toured the ship and watched Sea Harriers demonstrate take-offs and landings. With the minister having returned to Culdrose, *Invincible* set course south for Gibraltar at the head of the task group.

While *Invincible* and her group were in the Mediterranean trouble had flared in Lebanon where local militias were attacking US and British forces who were there on 'peacekeeping' duties during the bloody civil war and even bloodier Israeli military occupation of part of the country. It was no coincidence that while *Invincible* was in the eastern Mediterranean, her sister *Illustrious* and *Hermes* were arriving in the western Mediterranean for the NATO exercise 'Display Determination', which began as *Invincible* started her first transit of the Suez Canal. In the Indian Ocean *Invincible* exercised with a US Navy battle group, which included the 61,000-ton aircraft carrier *Ranger*. Harriers from the British carrier were able to carry out cross-deck training with *Ranger* and hundreds of US sailors crowded the island to watch the unusual sight of Lt-Cdr Tony Ogilvy, 801 Squadron's Commanding Officer, and Lt Richard Hawkins landing their aircraft vertically on the US carrier's flight deck. In mid-October, in company with *Aurora* and RFAs *Appleleaf, Olmeda* and *Regent, Invincible* made a four-day call at Bombay (Mumbai), where great interest was shown in both the ship and in the Sea Harrier aircraft. Among visitors to *Invincible* were the Indian Minister of Defence, six Indian Navy admirals and a delegation of senior officers from the Indian aircraft carrier, *Vikrant**. When *Invincible* left Bombay she had on board the Indian Defence Minister and the Chief of Staff of the Indian Navy, who watched displays by both Sea Harriers and Sea Kings. As a direct result of *Invincible's* visit to the Indian port, in May 1987 the Indian Navy would purchase HMS *Hermes,* together with Sea King and Sea Harrier aircraft. Nine days after leaving India, the carrier, in company with *Aurora, Rothesay* and the three RFAs, secured alongside Singapore's Sembawang Dockyard on the island's north shore. *Rothesay,* as the 'old lady' of the group, had once been stationed at the dockyard when it was the main naval base for the Royal Navy's Far East Station. After carrying out self-maintenance at Singapore, *Invincible* and her group left for the highlight of the deployment, a series of visits to Australian, New Zealand and Japanese ports. Unfortunately, they were to be marred by controversy.

After leaving Singapore *Invincible* and her group sailed through the islands of the Indonesian archipelago, where the traditional Crossing the Line ceremony took place. Not only was Captain Hill-Norton required to submit to King Neptune's attentions, but so was one member of the ship's company who was unwise enough to boast that in all his 19 years' service he had never had a ducking. As the group approached Fremantle, the first port of call, it 'gatecrashed' a joint US and RAN force carrying out an amphibious exercise, with the Sea Harriers carrying out surprise 'attacks' on the three US Navy assault ships and their Australian escorts. As always when Royal Navy ships visited antipodean ports *Invincible* and her group were given the traditional warm welcome in Fremantle, with wide coverage by the Australian press and television. It was after leaving Fremantle that the first problems arose, which would eventually have a direct effect on the ship's itinerary when, during exercises with Australian and New Zealand units, excessive vibration was encountered in the port propeller shaft bearings. Although the carrier's immediate

operational performance was not affected it was clear that the ship would require dry docking, and the obvious place for such work to be carried out was the Royal Australian Navy's dockyard at Sydney's Garden Island. This would also fit in well with the ship's Christmas visit to the city.

Meanwhile, as *Invincible* steamed towards New Zealand she played a key role in the rescue of the crew of a yacht which was in trouble in heavy seas off Australia's south-west coast. Later, as she sailed across the Tasman Sea, heading for the New Zealand capital of Wellington, there came a diplomatic decision which would lead to the first alteration in the carrier's itinerary. It had been planned that *Invincible's* New Year would be celebrated in Hong Kong, but with diplomatic negotiations over the colony's future at a delicate stage it was thought that a visit might adversely affect the talks, and so Hong Kong was struck off the carrier's schedule.

On 25 November, as *Invincible* sailed into Wellington's picturesque hill-lined harbour, she encountered the first protests by anti-nuclear campaigners, but these were far outweighed by the warmth of the welcome from the city's residents. During the four-day stopover there were sporting contests, personal reunions and hundreds of invitations to ship's company members. When *Invincible* was opened to the public the queue to get on board stretched for over a mile, and over 8,000 people visited the ship. On two evenings a colour guard from the carrier received an enthusiastic reception when they took part in the Wellington Tattoo on the city's Test cricket ground. It was while *Invincible* was at Wellington that the decision was made to cut short the carrier's visit to Auckland in order that she could be dry docked for repairs to her propeller shaft bearing. During the passage between Wellington and Auckland *Invincible* was escorted by HMNZS *Canterbury,* and she carried out an air defence exercise in conjunction with the Royal New Zealand Air Force. The welcome at Auckland on 30 November was enthusiastic, but there was also a small flotilla of boats containing anti-nuclear protesters. Although the protest did not disrupt the usual warm hospitality afforded by the people of Auckland to the Royal Navy, it was a portent of what was to come from an unexpected source - the Australian Government. During her stay in Auckland *Invincible* opened her gangway to some 18,000 visitors, one of whom was the Prime Minister of New Zealand.

When *Invincible* left Auckland her itinerary, which was to include Christmas at Sydney as well as visits to Singapore and Japan, was eagerly anticipated by the ship's company. However, in early December the carrier was suddenly thrust into the headlines of the world's press when the Australian Government, in response to the British Government's decision to neither confirm nor deny the existence of

* INS *Vikrant* was ex-HMS *Hercules*, a light fleet carrier which never served with the Royal Navy.

Invincible enters the port of Fremantle on 5 November 1983.

(Vic Jeffery, Royal Australian Navy)

nuclear weapons on board *Invincible,* refused the aircraft carrier access to the dry docking facilities at Sydney. The diplomatic row did not mar Sydney's traditional enthusiastic welcome given to all Royal Navy units, and as she moored in Woolloomooloo Bay the ship's company had easy access to the city centre. On Christmas Day 800 members of the carrier's company were invited to the homes of local people, and such was the hospitality that at one stage there were not enough off-watch sailors to respond to invitations. When *Invincible* was opened to the public over 12,000 people visited her; clearly, despite the politics, the Navy was as popular as ever in Australia.

As a result of the Australian Government's decision it was decided that in early January 1984 *Invincible* would go to Sembawang Dockyard in Singapore to undergo her dry docking and repairs. However, no sooner had that decision been made than the Japanese Prime Minister made the announcement that Japan would not accept a visit from *Invincible* because it was thought she was carrying nuclear weapons. Although the Australian Government had to a certain extent backed down on its original stance, the decision to use Singapore's dockyard was adhered to. The attitude taken by the Governments of Australia and Japan should be seen as a sign of the times in the Pacific region, which had over the years been used by the USA, Britain and France as a testing ground for nuclear weapons.

In the event *Invincible's* company spent an enjoyable Christmas in Sydney, and on 29 December when she left for Singapore by way of Australia's west coast, there were cheers and a few tears as well as she sailed out of Sydney Heads. On 9 January 1984 *Invincible* entered the former King George VI graving dock in Singapore's Sembawang Dockyard, where she would remain for the best part of the month. During this period the squadrons disembarked to the Singapore Air Force bases at Paya Lebar, which was formerly the island's main civil airport, and Sembawang, which had once been a Fleet Air Arm base. She also received a visit from the C-in-C Fleet who toured the ship, meeting officers and men, and presented a trophy to the ship's assistant canteen manager, in recognition of his excellent contribution to the life of the carrier, both during and after the Falklands War. By early February the work on *Invincible's* propeller shaft had been completed and she was able to take part in joint exercises with the US Navy in the South China Sea, off the Philippines. It soon became apparent, however, that the vibration problems had not been completely cured and it was decided to cancel a planned visit to Pusan and send *Invincible* home early so that the mechanical problem could be investigated fully and repaired. In the event she arrived home in Portsmouth on 20 March 1984, where she was given a rousing welcome from thousands of family members. She had been away for some six and a half months, during which time she had sailed 37,000 miles. The disruptions to the planned

programme had caused some disappointments on board, but despite this and some unwelcome publicity in the press, the deployment had been a success.

In early April 1984, with 50 sons of ship's company members on board, *Invincible* made the passage from Portsmouth to Devonport to begin a dockyard assisted refit which would last for two months. During this period the ship's port propeller shaft was replaced and all the main machinery was thoroughly overhauled. Following the completion of the work in mid-summer she underwent successful full-power trials in the Channel, when it seemed that her recurring propeller shaft problem had been cured. The remainder of 1984 was spent in home waters, and in early October she met the youngest of the three sisters, *Ark Royal,* which had put to sea for contractors' sea trials. While *Ark Royal* was at sea *Invincible* also took the opportunity to visit the Tyne, where she secured in her younger sister's berth in Walker Naval Yard. The visit allowed her to renew links with her affiliated city of Durham, and this time the principal event was the laying up of the ship's Falklands Battle Ensign in Durham Cathedral. Some 250 members of the ship's company, including Rear-Admiral J. J. Black and a dozen ex-*Invincibles*, marched through the city to take part in the service, which ended with a civic lunch in the Town Hall.

The new year of 1985 saw *Invincible* leave Portsmouth on 17 January, with a snow-covered flight deck, to spend a work-up period with her squadrons in a rough and bitterly cold North Sea, during which she played host to the C-in-C Fleet and the US Navy's Deputy C-in-C Naval Forces Europe. A proposed visit to Copenhagen during the last week of January was cancelled due to sub-zero temperatures and thick ice in the Baltic. Compensation came in the form of a visit to Rotterdam which, with a berth close to the city centre, proved to be just as popular. Although she would remain in home waters for most of 1985, it would be an extremely busy year for *Invincible* during which she would take a part in six major naval exercises.

The first of these began in February in thick Channel fog off Portland and in the South West Approaches, in company with the frigates *Lowestoft* and *Phoebe.* During this exercise 801 Squadron carried out a sustained period of flying and 820 Squadron were employed in their anti-submarine role. There followed a short break when the carrier visited Hamburg, then a few days later she took part in 'Exercise Cold Winter', which lived up to its name. This NATO amphibious, maritime, land and air exercise involved forces from the UK, Netherlands and Norway in the North Sea, Norwegian Sea and the coastal areas of Norway. Operating with *Fearless, Glamorgan, Jupiter, Newcastle* and *Yarmouth, Invincible's* task was to embark 450 Royal Marines of 45 Commando and transport them to the north of Norway, where they were landed in a helicopter-borne assault. Without any spare

A very smart *Invincible* enters Fremantle Harbour on 5 November 1983.

(Vic Jeffery, Royal Australian Navy)

An aerial view of *Invincible* as she enters Sydney Harbour on 12 December 1983.　　　*(Vic Jeffery, Royal Australian Navy)*

accommodation for commandos, many men slept on camp beds in ship's company mess decks, recreation spaces, the hangar and any other corner they could find. The landings took place in the very north of Norway, close to the border with Russia, and so it was expected that the Soviet Fleet would be much in evidence but, apart from 'Coot' and 'Bear' surveillance aircraft which overflew the exercise area, there was little sign of Soviet forces. At the end of the exercise, when *Invincible* set course south for Portsmouth, she had on board 29 aircraft: seven Sea King Mk V ASW helicopters, five Sea Harriers, six Gazelle helicopters, six Lynx helicopters, two Wessex helicopters and three Sea King Mk IV helicopters, which made for a very congested hangar and flight deck.

Following Easter leave and maintenance in Portsmouth *Invincible*, together with *Battleaxe, Glamorgan, Nottingham, Phoebe* and HM submarine *Olympus*, took part in Staff

College Sea Days in the Channel, during which hundreds of VIPs, MPs and foreign dignitaries were given an insight into naval operations. These were followed by a visit to Amsterdam and by 'Exercise Hardy Crab' in the South Western Approaches, when five RAF GR3 Harriers from 1(F) Squadron, together with 70 RAF support personnel, were embarked. The ship then provided air support for 3 Commando Brigade who were operating on Dartmoor and Bodmin Moor. With that exercise over *Invincible* sailed north for Rosyth Navy Days, where it was estimated that some 16,000 visitors toured the ship. No sooner were Navy Days over than *Invincible* was taking part in the NATO exercise code-named 'Roebuck', which also included Dutch and Belgian units, as well as *Scylla, Yarmouth*, RFA *Grey Rover* and men of the RAF Regiment. The exercise took the carrier into the North Sea and Pentland Firth and, for the ocean phase, into the Atlantic Ocean. Whilst the carrier

With Sydney Harbour Bridge providing the backdrop, *Invincible* is manoeuvred to her berth in the harbour.

(Vic Jeffery, Royal Australian Navy)

was off the Orkney Islands the Duke of Kent spent five hours on board watching flying operations and firing the Vulcan Phalanx anti-missile gun. On 10 July the ship provided the venue for 11 aircraft of the Helicopter Club of Great Britain before she returned to Portsmouth for leave, maintenance and to take part in Navy Days.

In the first week of September *Invincible* left Portsmouth to make the short passage west to Plymouth Sound, where she joined a large amphibious force for 'Exercise Rolling Deep'. In the Sound, on a bright, sunny and warm day, the carrier embarked elements of 42 Commando and a platoon of Spanish Marines before sailing at the head of the amphibious group, which included *Intrepid, Sir Lancelot, Sir Percivale,* MVs *England* and *Mercandian,* (two vessels which had been taken up from trade), the escort destroyer *Fife* and RFA *Olmeda.* The group sailed north by way of Ireland's west coast, with the passage being opposed by a nuclear submarine and attacking RAF Buccaneer aircraft. *Invincible's* Sea Harriers joined a mixed fighter force with Phantoms and Danish F16s to provide the air defence capability. By the time the force reached the landing area close to the Kyle of Lochalsh

the warm sunny weather had given way to high winds, heavy seas and torrential rain, but, nevertheless, 42 Commando and their Spanish counterparts were landed by 845 and 846 Squadron's Wessex and Sea King helicopters. Faced with appalling weather, however, it was considered that little would be gained from this phase of the exercise and the commandos were re-embarked some 24 hours earlier than had been planned. The second phase of 'Rolling Deep' took the task group to the Cape Wrath area, harried en route by two German submarines and RAF Buccaneers. By this time the amphibious group were facing storm force winds and more torrential rain, but on 17 September in the sheltered waters of Loch Eriboll, the commando force made another helicopter-borne landing ashore, allowing *Invincible* to sail into more open waters. Throughout the exercise one of Russia's modern spy ships took great interest in the proceedings, no doubt interested in any changes to British amphibious landing techniques following the Falklands War. On the way south 820 Squadron disembarked to Prestwick and aircraft from Brawdy, Chivenor and Yeovilton 'attacked' the carrier in a final air defence exercise. With the commandos having

Invincible meets *Ark Royal*, the youngest of the three sisters, for the first time on 1 October 1984.

(Fleet Air Arm Museum)

With the newly built *Ark Royal* at sea for her Contractor's Sea Trials, on 2 October 1984 *Invincible* took the opportunity to fill her berth at Walker Naval Yard, Newcastle upon Tyne. *(Brian Hargreaves)*

disembarked, *Invincible* returned to the Hebrides area for Sea Dart firings.

The last exercise of 1985, which took place in November, was code-named 'Iles d'Or' and, as the name suggests, was hosted by the French Navy. Flying the flag of FO Third Flotilla, Rear-Admiral J. J. R. Oswald, *Invincible* sailed south to Gibraltar and on into the Mediterranean to Toulon. During the passage she exercised with the submarine *Splendid,* and in the early stages of the exercise *Invincible,* with 820 Squadron, concentrated on anti-submarine warfare, thus providing protection for the French strike carrier *Foch.* Meanwhile, the Sea Harriers of 801 Squadron operated from *Foch* alongside French Super Entendard aircraft, providing air defences against the opposing A6s and Sky Warriors from USS *Coral Sea.* Halfway through the exercise *Invincible* had to rescue one of 820 Squadron's Sea Kings which had suffered a major oil leak some 80 miles from the carrier. The pilot managed to land the helicopter gently onto the water where its air flotation bags prevented an immediate sinking. The crew were quickly rescued by another Sea King, but the stricken helicopter capsized and began to settle in the water.

Fortunately, *Invincible's* diving team quickly came to the rescue and attached more flotation bags, but there then came the tricky task of recovering the aircraft which was actually lying upside down just below the surface of the sea. For 11 hours *Invincible* manoeuvred alongside the aircraft while recovery teams worked round the clock to attach lines to the Sea King, which had to be righted and drained of water before it could be hoisted safely onto the flight deck. Finally, with the exercise over, *Invincible* set course for Portsmouth where, after flying off her squadrons, she secured alongside and prepared to take on a new role.

When *Invincible* left Portsmouth on 14 January 1986, instead of Sea Harriers and Sea Kings on the flight deck, there were two large temporary classrooms in the form of Portakabins, as well as an assortment of road vehicles from minibuses and a smart Rover 800 saloon car to a Royal Navy presentation caravan. In the hangar the only aircraft were three Wessex helicopters of 845 Squadron. For the final weeks before undergoing her first major refit *Invincible* had taken on the role of a Dartmouth Training Ship, and for the deployment she embarked 217 young officers under training and 78 marine engineering artificer

A busy flight deck during Rosyth Navy Days, 8 June 1985. *(Brian Hargreaves)*

Invincible alongside at Rosyth for Navy Days in June 1985. *(Brian Hargreaves)*

RAS with HMS *Minerva* in January 1986, during her training cruise in the Caribbean.   (*Steve Wiseman*)

apprentices from HMS *Sultan*. Escorted by HMS *Minerva*, which had left Devonport on the same day, the carrier was bound for the Caribbean and a two-month deployment in the sun. One of the Artificer Apprentices on board was Steve Wiseman, who remembers that with no squadron personnel on board most of the ship's company had taken the opportunity to 'upgrade' their accommodation, with chief petty officers occupying empty junior officers' cabins and this was carried down the line to junior ratings who took over petty officers' mess decks. As for the MEA Apprentices he recalls: 'I was living in 7G mess, which had formerly been the ship's library and it had been allocated to the apprentices whose surnames began with W. All the rest were put down in the larger 6G mess decks. The Officers Under Training, or OUTs, were soon referred to as Sub Lieutenants Under Training, which inevitably became shortened to SLUTs.'

The first few days of the transatlantic passage were marked by severe gales, but after the short stop at Ponta Delgada in the Azores the weather improved and it was not long before tropical whites became the rig of the day. For the Officers under Training there were astronavigational lessons, small arms and guard drills, close-weapons shoots, seaboat drills and Officer of the Watch manoeuvres. The apprentices meanwhile, although their sea training was centred around the Engine Room Department, were formed up into groups, and sent off to different departments so that they could learn more about the operational running of the ship. All the trainees undertook light jackstay transfers with *Minerva* and flights in the Wessex helicopters. During off-watch hours there were deck sports, and the flight deck was soon being protected from corrosion by a covering of well-oiled bodies worshipping the sun.

Invincible enters Bridgetown Harbour, Barbados, on 24 January 1986.   *(Steve Wiseman)*

On 24 January, ten days out of Portsmouth, while *Minerva* detached for a visit to St Lucia, *Invincible* secured alongside at Bridgetown, Barbados, and everyone on board was able to spend off-watch time in a variety of ways from enjoying the sun-drenched beaches to sampling the cheap and plentiful rum cocktails. Sadly, on the final full day of the visit a member of the ship's company, LWEM Stephen Barr, was the victim of a hit and run road accident and he subsequently died of his injuries. This tragedy cast a shadow over the visit, particularly as the unfortunate rating was married with two young daughters. Next day, 29 January, *Invincible* left Bridgetown to rendezvous with *Minerva* and begin a phase of coastal navigation round Barbados and on to the Grenadines, where the beautiful Holisborough Bay, Cariacou, provided a popular beach for banyans. Over two days at anchor more than 1,000 men were landed so that they could enjoy beach barbecues with musical accompaniment from the Royal Marines Band of FO Third Flotilla. Following this popular stopover both *Invincible* and *Minerva* continued north to their respective destinations of Antigua and Grenada, with *Invincible*

spending five days in English Harbour, Antigua, an island reputed to have 365 palm-fringed beaches of golden sand. There was also the additional attraction of watching the visiting England cricket team which was on the island to play a match against the Leeward Islands side. Both teams were invited on board and the England Captain, David Gower, presented Captain Kit Layman with an autographed cricket bat which was to be raffled in order to raise money for the family of LWEM Barr. It was generally agreed that the five days spent at Antigua passed far too quickly, and on 11 February *Invincible* was at sea again with *Minerva,* setting course for Fort Lauderdale. This visit lasted for eight days, which gave an opportunity to grant both watches a few days' leave. Most had a chance to see the Everglades or Disney World, while a few travelled as far afield as Tampa, Washington and even California. Before leaving Fort Lauderdale *Invincible* and *Minerva* were joined by HMS *Apollo,* and when the carrier entered Nassau on 26 February to secure close to three luxury cruise ships, she was flying the flag of the C-in-C Fleet, Admiral Sir Nicholas Hunt. Once again, on this sun-drenched island,

A very smart 'Procedure Alpha' during *Invincible*'s training cruise. The Portakabins on the flight deck are actually classrooms for the sub lieutenants under training; the two Wessex helicopters ranged on deck were the only aircraft on board during the deployment. *(Steve Wiseman)*

A close-up of *Invincible* at her fitting-out berth, showing the uncluttered lines of her stern and port side. *(Brian Hargreaves)*

The old and the new. On 2 May 1980 *Invincible* visited Devonport where she met the old fleet carrier HMS *Ark Royal* which was laid up and awaiting her final trip to the shipbreaker's yard.

(Fleet Air Arm Museum)

Surrounded by an armada of small craft of every description, on 17 September 1982 *Invincible* returned to Portsmouth in triumph from her vital role in the South Atlantic.

(Fleet Air Arm Museum)

A view of *Invincible* as she is manoeuvred to her berth in Sydney Harbour.

(Ross Gillett OAM, Royal Australian Navy)

Invincible arrives in Sydney on 12 December 1983.

(Ross Gillett, Royal Australian Navy)

'Clear lower deck of families and friends'. *Invincible* puts to sea for a Families Day on 3 August 1984.

(Walter Sartori)

An impressive bow view of *Invincible* under way in Portsmouth Harbour.

(Derek Fox)

An aerial view of *Invincible* at sea.

Invincible and her sister *Illustrious* at sea together.   *(Fleet Air Arm Museum)*

A fine view of *Invincible* as she passes Southsea Common and the funfair as she makes her way into Portsmouth Harbour.   *(Fleet Air Arm Museum)*

Invincible passes the Statue of Liberty as she enters New York Harbour on 1 July 2004, for a six-day visit following her participation in 'Exercise Aurora'.
(MOD Crown Copyright)

With her ship's company and trainees manning the flight deck, *Invincible* approaches Fort Lauderdale, Florida, on 17 February 1986. (*Steve Wiseman*)

73

Invincible entering Portsmouth Harbour on her return from the Caribbean on 18 March 1986.　　　　*(Walter Sartori)*

the beaches provided some cheaper entertainment for the ship's company, whilst a group of apprentices repaired a bus and generator at a children's hostel, as well as replacing old electrical wiring and fixing furniture and toys. They ended the day by treating the children to a barbecue. *Invincible* left Nassau at 06.00 on 1 March and, after completing a mini-flying display at a local air show, with *Apollo, Minerva* and RFA *Pearleaf,* she sailed for the US Navy's Atlantic Fleet Weapons Range off Puerto Rico. Arriving off the range on 4 March *Invincible* provided an impressive display when her Sea Dart missiles hit and totally destroyed their target. It was, however, the end of the deployment and after a 13-day transatlantic crossing, on 17 March *Invincible* arrived at her home base of Portsmouth.

Before her long refit began *Invincible* had just one final operational duty to perform, and between 7 and 18 April she anchored in the Solent mining ground where she was used as a 'test bed' for underwater explosion trials. These consisted of a series of explosions which were detonated close to the ship in order to test the effectiveness of her machinery and equipment in a wartime environment. Although she was subjected to only five explosions, and no more than one explosion on any day, the cloud of smoke and spray from the underwater mines appeared at times to almost envelope the ship. On 28 April 1986, however, the tests were concluded and *Invincible* left the Solent to set course for Devonport, where she arrived alongside the next day. Since commissioning in 1980 she had clocked up 260,000 miles, and had received over 250,000 visitors, but it would be late 1988 before *Invincible* was at sea again.

Invincible joins the cruise ships *Festivale*, *Carnivale* and *Royale* at Nassau, Bahamas, on 27 February 1986. (*Steve Wiseman*)

Chapter Five

A New Look
May 1986 – November 1992

S oon after her arrival at Devonport Dockyard on 29 April 1986, *Invincible's* complement was reduced to 200 as she prepared for a two-and-a-half-year, £120 million modernization refit. The work included the installation of improved command and control facilities in the Operations Room which was itself substantially rebuilt, together with the main communications office and computer room. The accommodation for a larger 21-aircraft air group, including a briefing room, squadron offices and storage for aircraft spares, was provided; varying according to the ship's role at any given time, the group would typically consist of eight Sea Harriers and 12 Sea Kings. The ship's self-defence capabilities were improved by the addition of three Goalkeeper close-in weapons, each of which was capable of firing some 4,200 rounds a minute. They were positioned forward, aft and midships in order to give overlapping arcs of fire and reduce the obstruction to aircraft. In addition to these new weapons an improved Seagnat chaff dispensing system, improved Type 996 radar, Type 2016 sonar and electronic support measures were

fitted, as well as a steeper 12° ski-ramp which improved the Sea Harriers' endurance by allowing them to take off from a shorter run. This in turn offered greater deck space for aircraft parking and helicopter operations. One of the biggest tasks was the replacement of hydraulic lift locks on the forward aircraft lift with electrically operated equipment. This entailed lifting the 42-ton platform clear of the ship and the removal of four giant five-hundredweight pins, to release the lift from its scissor-action operating gear.

It was in November 1988 when *Invincible* left Devonport to undergo her preliminary post-refit trials and gale force winds kept her at sea for longer than scheduled. Further trials were held the following month during which, for the first time since April 1986, a Sea King of 826 Squadron landed on board. Final contractors' sea trials were carried out in February 1989 and in March that year flying trials were conducted in the Channel with the Sea Harriers of 801 Squadron. Her return to her home port of Portsmouth saw the three sisters, *Invincible, Illustrious* and

Invincible at sea on exercises.
(Fleet Air Arm Museum)

Sea Harriers landing on board *Invincible* at sea.

Ark Royal, together for the first time. Finally, during the afternoon of Thursday 18 May 1989, in the presence of her royal sponsor, *Invincible* was recommissioned. Having visited HMS *Dolphin* during the forenoon, Her Majesty the Queen made her way by royal barge to *Invincible* where, to the crashing of a 21-gun salute, she was met by Captain Michael Gretton, the carrier's commanding officer. The ceremony was held in the hangar, which was packed with over 2,000 members of the ship's company, their relatives and friends. After the recommissioning ceremony a magnificent cake was cut by Mrs Stephanie Gretton, the commanding officer's wife, assisted by JS John Newcombe, the carrier's youngest rating. Later the Queen toured the ship and met members of the ship's company and their families. As a memento of the day Captain Gretton presented the Queen with a framed colour photograph of *Invincible* leaving Devonport after her refit, and as the royal party left the carrier there was a fly-past of *Invincible's* new air group, made up of the Sea Harriers of 800 Squadron, the Sea Kings of 814 Squadron and the airborne early warning Sea Kings of 849A Flight.

After recommissioning *Invincible* completed her equipment trials and began a series of work-ups which were designed to bring her up to a fully operational state. Her air group joined for flying training in the North Western Approaches, and off the coast of Scotland she enjoyed the distinction of hosting part of the first ever visit by a Soviet Minister of Defence to a NATO country. It was a sign of the rapidly changing political scene in Eastern Europe, and the Russian General Dmitri Yazov, accompanied by a delegation of senior officers, was flown on board from Stornaway. The visitors were given a presentation in Russian about the ship, which was followed by a flying display with a demonstration of live depth charges and 1,000lb bombs. *Invincible* spent several weeks in the area of the North Western Approaches, during which she undertook Area Capability Training, and both the ship and her air group were able to operate against surface, air and submarine threats in a deep water environment. In July, with her Operational Readiness Inspection having been successfully completed, the carrier sailed south to the picturesque port of Vigo in north-west Spain. Here the ship's company was able to relax with sports fixtures against local teams, regular coach trips to fine local beaches or excursions to local attractions, with of course, ample opportunities to sample the local wine.

With summer leave over *Invincible* continued to operate in home waters, receiving visits from the Defence Secretary and, more popularly, from two actresses who were starring in 'Coronation Street'. In the autumn of 1989, in company with the destroyer *Cornwall, Invincible* crossed the Atlantic for a WESTLANT (Western Atlantic) deployment to the eastern coast of the USA. As well as spending Christmas and New Year in the United States, the carrier exercised her anti-submarine capabilities in the Atlantic Ocean and fired her missiles in the Puerto Rican exercise areas. After visiting Fort Lauderdale and the US Naval Base at Norfolk, Virginia, she took part in a major American exercise code-named 'Fleetex', which began off Norfolk and ended two weeks later in the area off Puerto Rico. She spent five weeks alongside at Mayport undergoing maintenance, which also took in the Christmas and New Year holiday periods, during which time the squadrons deployed to US bases ashore, and before returning home to Portsmouth at the end of February 1990, she also managed a visit to Barbados.

After only ten days at her home port *Invincible* was at sea again, this time heading north for the bitterly cold waters of northern Norway and the Arctic Circle, to take part in the appropriately named amphibious exercise, 'Cold Winter'. Other British units taking part in the Norwegian exercise included *Intrepid, Alacrity, Amazon* and *Hermione,* as well as the RFAs *Sir Bedivere, Sir Percivale, Sir Tristram* and *Olmeda.* HMS *Herald* provided mine countermeasures support, while the embarked force in *Invincible* included elements of 42 and 45 Commandos, together with Dutch Marines. *Invincible's* usual air group of Sea Harriers and Sea Kings disembarked for this exercise and they were replaced by the Mk IV Sea Kings of 845 and 846 Squadrons. Two of the helicopters sailed with the ship from Portsmouth and six joined at Andalsnes in central Norway, where they assisted with the embarkation of over 500 men, together with their guns and equipment. The last six helicopters of 846 Squadron joined the ship at Vestfjord and having carried out landing rehearsals, the force moved under cover of darkness to Malangen Fjord, south of Tromso and well inside the Arctic Circle. Having landed her troops *Invincible* remained in the fjord acting as an operating base, and during this time she had a lucky escape from what could have been a disaster. Early one morning the carrier's port anchor cable parted and, very gently, the ship grounded on the fjord's only mud bank where, with part of her bilge keel embedded, she remained firmly stuck. Ship's divers from both *Invincible* and *Intrepid* were soon sent down and they were quickly able to establish that the propellers and rudder were clear of the mud, and that damage had been limited to superficial scratches. Later, with the assistance of the tug *Nimble* and three of *Intrepid's* LCUs, the carrier was refloated and she was able to resume her role in the exercise. Three days later 500 men of 45 Commando and an Air Defence Battery, together with their equipment and guns, were flown back to the ship for passage to Arbroath. *Invincible* then sailed south to Portsmouth to spend a month alongside undergoing maintenance.

The spring of 1990 saw *Invincible* sailing south to the warmer climes of the Mediterranean and the annual NATO exercise, 'Dragon Hammer'. In addition to

Invincible at sea off Portland.

A bitterly cold day north of the Arctic Circle, but the Sea King in the foreground remains cheerful.

(Fleet Air Arm Museum)

Invincible four other aircraft carriers took part, including the giant USS *Eisenhower* and the smaller USS *Saipan,* as well as the Italian and Spanish vessels *Garibaldi* and *Principe de Asturias* respectively. In addition to the carriers ten amphibious ships, eight submarines and 20 destroyers and frigates from seven NATO countries took part in the exercise, together with a wide range of aircraft operating from bases in Italy, France, Spain, Sardinia and Sicily. After a two-day settling down phase, the main naval forces moved through the Sicilian Channel to allow marines from the UK, USA, France, Spain and Italy to make amphibious landings on the north-west coast of Sicily. After briefings in Cadiz between officers from *Invincible* and *Principe de Asturias,* the two carriers worked closely together during the exercise and cross-deck operations were conducted between the two ships, with *Invincible's* Sea Harriers and Sea Kings operating from *Principe de Asturias,* and AV8B Matadors from the Spanish carrier operating from *Invincible.* With groups of maintenance engineers exchanging ships for short periods, good relations were

quickly established. The Sea Harriers of 800 Squadron also operated from the Italian carrier *Garibaldi.* Sadly, during the exercise one of 800 Squadron's pilots, Lt Stephen Holmes, died when his aircraft crashed into the sea off Sardinia while taking part in an early morning sortie. Although a search was mounted and wreckage was found, there was no trace of the pilot and a memorial service for him was held on board. In the event *Invincible* did not see the end of the exercise for, suffering from mechanical problems in her propeller shaft bearings, she cut short her participation and returned home to Portsmouth for repair work to be carried out.

It was early May 1990 when *Invincible* returned to sea for trials and to serve as the flagship of Rear-Admiral Peter Woodhead for Staff College Sea Days. Operating with *Coventry, Manchester, Nottingham,* the submarine *Onyx* and HMS *Brocklesbury,* the carrier was able to demonstrate naval operations to over 400 visitors. With the demonstrations completed *Invincible* paid her first visit to London, as she manoeuvred slowly upriver and through the

Invincible at Sunderland,
29 June 1990.
(Brian Hargreaves)

Thames Barrier to Greenwich where, with the old Royal Naval College providing a backdrop, she secured to a buoy. During the visit, as well as providing opportunities for runs ashore in the capital, members of the ship's company took time out to take part in various charity fundraising events. In addition to groups of handicapped children being entertained on board, money was raised for the British Heart Foundation and, as the visit came to an end, a team of cyclists from the ship's AEW flight set off on a sponsored bike ride to Sunderland to raise money for a children's cancer charity. During her summer leave and maintenance period at Portsmouth *Invincible* was host ship to the visiting Russian destroyer *Bezuprechny,* whose five days in port concluded with a concert on *Invincible's* flight deck by the band and dancers of the Soviet Northern Fleet.

The late summer and autumn of 1990 saw *Invincible* back in the North Sea for a visit to Sunderland followed by 'Exercise Teamwork' in company with *Ark Royal, Liverpool, Manchester, Intrepid, Sheffield, Coventry, Brilliant, Ambuscade, Arrow* and *Argonaut.* Some 85 ships from eight nations took part in amphibious exercises which took them to Norwegian waters, in the area around Namsos as well as to the old wartime anchorage at Scapa Flow. Although the exercise was much reduced owing to the first Gulf War, it included convoy protection, anti-submarine warfare and amphibious landings. Later in the year, on 29 November 1990, *Invincible* made naval history when she became the first Royal Navy unit to embark WRNS personnel as part of her ship's company. Several mess decks on No 6 deck

had been converted for the accommodation of female members of her complement and, as more women began to serve with the fleet at sea, more self-contained mess decks were added on both No 5 and No 6 decks forward.

The early months of 1991 saw *Invincible,* together with the destroyer *Edinburgh,* crossing the Atlantic for WESTLANT exercises with the US and Netherlands Navies. At one stage in the joint exercises *Invincible* operated with the Dutch frigate *Piet Heyn* against a US submarine and, while the two ships were in company, they exchanged female personnel for several hours. Before returning across the Atlantic to her home port of Portsmouth the carrier managed a visit to Bridgetown, Barbados. Later in the year, during early September, *Invincible,* together with other Royal Navy units, took part in 'Exercise Vendetta' in the North Atlantic and North Sea. This was followed by 'Exercise North Star', during which she flew the flag of Vice-Admiral Sir Nicholas Hill-Norton, one of her former commanding officers, who was now commander of NATO's anti-submarine strike force. Some 50 Royal Navy ships and 200 aircraft from six NATO countries took part, as well as the US Navy's strike carrier *America.* During the course of the exercise one of 814 Squadron's Sea King helicopters, which was operating from *Invincible,* made a controlled ditching in rough weather 40 miles west of the Shetland Islands. Fortunately, the crew were rescued uninjured by another helicopter, and the stricken aircraft was later located at a depth of 135 metres and successfully salvaged. Following this exercise *Invincible* moved south to the Mediterranean for the NATO exercise 'Display Determination', which also involved *Cumberland, Edinburgh* and RFAs *Fort George* and *Olwen. Invincible* then moved further east for three days of exercises with the Egyptian Navy off that country's coast, code-named 'Exercise Nile 91'. Under the command of Vice-Admiral Hill-Norton the Royal Navy's task group, together with Egyptian Navy units including *Abu Qir* and *El Suez,* tested most aspects of maritime warfare. The exercise culminated in a visit to the Egyptian port of Alexandria, where the carrier was the highlight of Egyptian Navy Days, and from where members of the ship's company attended an International Service of Commemoration at the Commonwealth War Graves Commission at El Alamein. Many Second World War veterans who attended the service were delighted to see *Invincible's* sailors lining the route through the cemetery to the Stone of Remembrance. There then followed a visit to Istanbul and on 31 October, during the passage to Sicily, *Invincible* and *Edinburgh* received a distress call from a large motor cruiser, MV *Ark,* which was in difficulties off the coast of Crete. Sea Kings from 814 Squadron were launched from the carrier and a small team led by Lt-Cdr Ian Beaumont landed on board the motor cruiser, before winching the occupants, including six women and two children, to safety. On board MV *Ark* a team of marine engineers began the difficult task of salvaging the vessel, but when she finally lost all power *Edinburgh* took her in tow to Kastellion on Crete's north-west coast. Following the rescue *Invincible* and *Edinburgh* rejoined *Fort Grange* and *Olwen* at Palermo, the next port of call on the deployment, which ended at Portsmouth on 18 November 1991.

With Christmas and New Year leave over, the first quarter of 1992 saw *Invincible* at sea carrying out Operational Sea Training off Portland, followed by 'Exercise Teamwork' in the North Atlantic. The highlight of the year for the aircraft carrier and her company was to be her 'Orient 92' deployment, which would take her, and a task group commanded by Rear-Admiral John Brigstocke, away to Far Eastern waters for six months. Leaving Portsmouth on 12 May *Invincible,* together with *Boxer, Newcastle* and *Norfolk, Fort Austin* and *Olwen,* set course for Gibraltar. With the Sea Harriers of 800 Squadron and the Sea Kings of 814 and 845 Squadrons embarked, the deployment was to be the longest and most ambitious 'out of area' since the withdrawal from the Far East Station in the early 1970s, and it was to be one of the most successful. After *Invincible* had passed Stromboli Island in the Tyrrhenian Sea, the first exercises were held in the eastern Mediterranean and these were followed by a run ashore at Piraeus. After making her southbound transit of the Suez Canal and leading an unsuccessful air and sea search for three missing crewmen from a merchant ship, MV *Ghazouet,* at the southern end of the Gulf of Aden

near Socotra Island, in deteriorating weather conditions *Invincible* left the area and set course for Mombasa.

On 14 June, during the passage south, *Invincible* crossed the equator, marking the event with due ceremony, and no sooner had she arrived in Mombasa's Kilindini Harbour than the Kenyan Wildlife Service requested help from the ship's helicopters to airlift building materials to a hilltop in Tsavo National Park. Most members of the ship's company were content to visit the unforgettable bars and clubs of Kilindini Road, which leads from the port gates into the town, and sample the delights of ice-cold Tusker Beer, as well as the long stretch of golden sandy beaches which runs from Nyali north to Kikambala. After leaving Mombasa *Invincible* and her group took part in 'Exercise Sea Copra', which involved an amphibious landing by 40 Commando on the Indian Ocean island of Diego Garcia. On 9 July *Invincible* arrived in Singapore's Sembawang Dockyard and four days later she sailed for Yokosuka in Japan, from where she took part in exercises with five units of Japan's Maritime Self Defence Force's Fourth Escort Group, which included the multi-purpose destroyer *Umigiri.* The manoeuvres began some 20 miles south of Tokyo Bay and included cross-deck operations between *Invincible's* Sea Kings and Japanese Sea Hawks. There were also simulated surface actions and air defence exercises and for a time Japan's Admiral Nitta embarked in the carrier. From Japan *Invincible* sailed to South Korea for a six-day visit to Pusan where she hosted a British Defence Trade Sales Exhibition in the hangar. From Pusan she set course for Hong Kong for a self-maintenance period and some leave, but with typhoons an ever-present threat the ship herself remained at short notice for sea in case she had to clear the harbour and ride out any storms well away from the coast.

In September *Invincible* took part in a 'Five Power' exercise in the South China Sea, which included units and aircraft from Australia, Malaysia, New Zealand, Singapore and the UK. 'Exercise Starfish' took the carrier into the South China Sea, where banyans at Pulau Tioman brought back nostalgic memories of service on the Far East Station in the late 1960s and early 1970s. During the 14-day exercise the Sea Harriers of 800 Squadron flew 96 sorties, integrating closely with RNZAF Sky Hawks and the Singapore Air Force's F16 Falcons and F5 Tigers. Meanwhile, 814 Squadron, who had transferred to RFA *Fort Austin,* provided anti-submarine protection for the force. On conclusion of the exercise, while *Boxer* sailed south to Australia, *Invincible* visited Georgetown, the principal town on the island of Penang. After leaving Penang the carrier began her homeward passage, via the Persian Gulf and the port of Abu Dhabi where she hosted another Defence Trade Sales Exhibition and over 80 guests toured the exhibits of 26 British companies which were displayed in the hangar. On 5 November *Invincible* made

Invincible at Sunderland on 26 September 1990.
(Brian Hargreaves)

her northbound transit of the Suez Canal and paid a visit to the old Arab port of Haifa, now part of Israel, before taking part in an air-defence exercise off Cyprus.

Sunday 22 November saw *Invincible* and her group leaving Gibraltar for the final leg of the deployment as they made their way home. The first day at sea saw one of 814 Squadron's Sea Kings make a successful emergency landing on the flight deck after its port engine caught fire, and next day the weather had deteriorated so much that flying operations were cancelled. On Tuesday 24 November, *Invincible* was ploughing through heavy seas and gale force winds in the Bay of Biscay when, at 08.20, a distress call was received from a 4,000-ton Danish merchantman, MV *Charm,* which was some 270 miles to the west of the carrier. With her cargo having shifted in the heavy sea, and having shipped some four metres of water, the freighter was in serious trouble and it was decided that *Invincible* should detach from the group and head westwards at maximum speed to get as close as possible to the stricken ship in order to launch her Sea Kings. At 10.20, however, came the news that the *Charm* had sunk with the loss of eight lives and a full-scale international search and rescue operation had been mounted. The Dutch frigate *Philips van Almonde*

picked up four bodies from the sea and another merchantman, MV *Horn,* rescued four survivors from a life raft. One of the men had suffered internal injuries and he was flown to *Invincible* for treatment. After a rough passage north, during the afternoon of Wednesday 25 November *Invincible* arrived in Falmouth Bay where the injured seaman was flown to Truro Hospital, and the stores and personnel of 814 Squadron were flown to Culdrose. At 10.00 the next day, as the ship was steaming east off Plymouth Sound, the Princess Royal, in her role as Chief Commandant of the WRNS, flew out to the carrier. Then, to the accompaniment of a fly-past by 800 Squadron's Sea Harriers and the carrier's Sea Kings, the other units of the group performed a traditional steam past and cheer ship, before detaching to their home ports. Next day, Friday 27 November, a cold, grey day, *Invincible* arrived alongside in Portsmouth Dockyard where not even the weather could dampen the enthusiasm of the welcome from hundreds of waiting families and friends.

Over a period of six months *Invincible* had sailed some 25,000 miles and the group as a whole had visited 29 ports in 20 countries.

Chapter Six

From the Adriatic to the Persian Gulf
December 1992 – November 1997

Upon *Invincible's* return to Portsmouth in November 1992, she was taken in hand for a dockyard assisted maintenance period which kept her out of service for four months. It was 27 March 1993 when she put to sea again to begin a shakedown period followed by Operational Sea Training at Portland and participation in Joint Maritime Course 932 in Scottish waters. During this period her air group consisted of 800 Squadron's Sea Harriers and the Sea Kings of 814 Squadron. With summer leave having been taken early, on 22 July 1993 *Invincible* left Portsmouth bound for the Mediterranean and the NATO task group which was deployed on 'Operation Grapple' in the Adriatic Sea. Taking over from *Ark Royal, Invincible* was to patrol the coast of the former Balkan state of Yugoslavia*, ready to support the United Nations peacekeeping forces ashore. *Ark Royal* had been on station for some seven months and before leaving the area she transferred one of her Sea Harriers to 800 Squadron in order to bring their strength up to seven. Because of operational requirements, when flying over Bosnia an additional Sea Harrier was needed. *Ark Royal* then returned to Portsmouth to give leave and to undergo maintenance. No sooner had *Invincible* arrived in the Adriatic than she hosted two VIP visits, the first by the Chief of the Defence Staff and the second by the Secretary of State for Defence.

During her Adriatic deployment *Invincible's* task group, which was under the command of Rear-Admiral M. P. Gretton, one of the carrier's former commanding officers, consisted of *Boxer, Beaver, Edinburgh,* the Dutch frigate *Jan van Brakel,* RFAs *Fort George* and *Olwen* and, in September, HMS *London. Invincible* also worked closely with the French aircraft carrier *Clemenceau* under an arrangement known as 'shared carrier tasking', which provided for either *Invincible* or *Clemenceau* to commit aircraft for 'Operation Deny Flight' over the former Yugoslavia. While one of the carriers enforced the no-fly zone and provided support for the United Nations troops ashore, the other was free to exercise elsewhere in the Mediterranean but it was always prepared to return at short notice, if necessary. These shared duties allowed the carriers to continue the essential process of maintaining their military capability when away from the

Adriatic. On 20 September *Invincible* was the venue for top secret peace talks between Muslim, Serb and Croat leaders in a conference which had been organized by the two international mediators, Lord Owen and Thorvald Stoltenberg. The meeting was attended by all the senior political figures from the separate states which had once formed Yugoslavia, including President Tudjman of Croatia, President Izetbegovic of Bosnia, Momcilo Krajisnik, the speaker of the Serb Parliament, and the controversial Bosnian Serb leader, Radovan Karadzic. The delegates were all flown on board by helicopter and it was hoped that the warring factions could be persuaded to sign a peace agreement, but in the event it was all in vain and the acrimonious conference broke up without any agreement being reached. As a result a signing ceremony in Sarajevo, which had been arranged between Serb, Croat and Muslim leaders, was abandoned.

For *Invincible's* ship's company the period in the Adriatic proved to be a testing time, particularly for the pilots of 800 Squadron who clocked up over 500 flying sorties over Bosnia. The Sea Harriers, which were operating in support of United Nations Resolutions, not only enforced the no-fly zone over Bosnia-Herzegovina, but they also provided close air support to the United Nations safe areas and anti-surface vessel combat air patrols in support of embargo operations and photographic reconnaissance missions. The flexibility of aircraft carriers allowed the vessels to manoeuvre to clear areas and to continue flying operations when shore bases were closed due to adverse weather conditions. There were, however, periods for rest and relaxation, when *Invincible* was able to stand down from her duties and visit ports in the region. Two of the most memorable visits were those to Corfu in September, and Valletta's Grand Harbour for Christmas and New Year. At the latter the Royal Navy's strong association with the island of Malta was still apparent, and when the carrier was opened to the public she proved to be a very popular attraction. *Invincible's* first tour of duty in the Adriatic came to an end in early February 1994 when she was relieved by *Ark Royal* and on 8 February she returned to Portsmouth to an enthusiastic welcome from

---

* Yugoslavia had come about as a result of the First World War, as a union of Serbia, Croatia, Slovenia, Montenegro and Bosnia-Herzegovina. It proclaimed itself as the Kingdom of Serbs, Croats and Slovenes on 1 December 1918 and it was always a very precarious alliance dominated by Serbia. It lasted for 72 years and collapsed in 1991 in bloody ethnic and religious rivalries which had been suppressed for years.

Alongside at Malta's Grand Harbour for Christmas 1993.   *(Michael Cassar)*

Visitors on *Invincible's* flight deck when she was opened to the public at Grand Harbour, December 1993.

(Michael Cassar)

thousands of relatives and friends crowded onto the jetty. She would now undergo a well-earned period of leave and maintenance.

Soon after arriving home *Invincible* received a visit from the first Deputy C-in-C of the Russian Navy, Admiral Igor Vladimerovich Kasatonov, who was paying an informal visit to Portsmouth Naval Base. It was another reminder of the sweeping changes which had affected the strategic situation in eastern Europe and it virtually signalled the end of *Invincible's* original role as a command ship for an anti-submarine force in the Atlantic Ocean. It was the early summer of 1994 before *Invincible* was at sea again undergoing her trials and work-up period with the improved FA2 Sea Harriers of 899 Squadron, which had embarked for their proving trials. On 24 August, however, she left Portsmouth bound for the Adriatic where, just over a week later, she relieved *Ark Royal*. During this deployment, in addition to 800 Squadron's FRS1 Sea Harriers, she had a flight of 801 Squadron's FA2 Sea Harriers, 814 Squadron's Sea Kings and the Sea Kings of

849A Flight. For the squadrons on board, *Invincible's* second stint in the Adriatic proved to be more eventful than the first and soon after her arrival in the area, as the aircraft began their 'Operation Deny Flight' patrols over Bosnia, two of the new FA2s came under fire from hand-held surface-to-air missiles over the town of Bihac, close to the border between Bosnia and Croatia. Both aircraft took evasive action and returned safely to the carrier, but it was a reminder of the dangerous situation in this volatile area of the Balkans, while the new FA2s were put to the test in operational conditions. At various times during the deployment *Invincible* led HM Ships *Brave, Brilliant, Campbeltown, Coventry* and *Cumberland,* as well as the RFAs *Fort Austin, Fort Grange* and *Olna,* and she also operated in conjunction with the Spanish aircraft carrier *Principe de Asturias.* During breaks from her patrols she made visits to Naples and Trieste, and from the former trips were arranged to Pompeii, Sorrento and Capri, while a group of 30 officers and ratings were given the opportunity to travel to Rome for an audience with the Pope. Ashore in

On 2 February 1994, *Ark Royal* took over the Bosnia Patrol from *Invincible*, which is ahead of her younger sister. *(Fleet Air Arm Museum)*

pilots were able to use metallic chaff decoys and electronic jamming as well as manoeuvring techniques in order to avoid the missiles which missed them by a wide margin and exploded above them. It was thought that these were fired in revenge for a NATO air attack on Udbina airfield in Serb-held Krajina the previous day. On 15 December a Sea Harrier pilot from *Invincible* ejected safely over the Adriatic Sea when his aircraft crashed some 15 miles north-east of Bari whilst on a training mission. He was rescued by a helicopter from the Spanish aircraft carrier *Principe de Asturias* and returned safely to *Invincible*. The aircraft was later recovered from a depth of 720 metres. Christmas and New Year were spent at Malta and at the end of February 1995, after being relieved by her younger sister *Illustrious, Invincible* returned to Portsmouth to undergo a dockyard assisted maintenance period.

During her period in Portsmouth Dockyard *Invincible* was dry docked in order that a new sewage treatment plant could be installed, a task which entailed cutting large holes in the ship's underwater hull, installing the caravan-sized plants and refitting the cutaway sections. Other improvements included new galley equipment and enhancements associated with the operation of the new FA2 Sea Harriers on board. After beginning her work-up in late May 1995 *Invincible* left home waters to begin her third period of duty in the Adriatic and some eight weeks later, after a busy few weeks off Bosnia, she called at Palma, Majorca, for a rest and maintenance period. At this time essential repairs were needed to her Type 1022 radar, which meant that for the first time the 2.5-tonne aerial was being removed outside a naval dockyard. However, her stay on the island was cut short by a renewed crisis in Bosnia, where fighting had broken out between Bosnian Serbs and Muslim forces with the result that NATO forces had launched a series of air strikes against the Bosnian Serbs. *Invincible's* urgent recall to the Adriatic meant round-the-clock work for the ship's weapons engineering staff in order to get the ship ready for sea, and she arrived off the coast of Bosnia during the early hours of 3 September.

With Bosnian Serb forces having lain siege to the city of Sarajevo, 800 Squadron's Sea Harriers took part in the NATO bombing campaign over Serb-held positions

Bosnia a small working party helped with the restoration of a shell-damaged school in Bugojna, near Gornji Vakuf, after which lessons were able to recommence. Whilst at sea the ship hosted many visitors, with exchange programmes being arranged with the Army ashore in Bosnia, the US Navy and even with the submarine *Tireless*. She also hosted visits from a number of VIPs, including the Second Sea Lord and a Government Minister.

In late November there was a more serious incident for two of 800 Squadron's Sea Harriers when, while on patrol over the Serb-occupied Bosnian city of Banja Luka, they came under fire from Sam-2 radio-guided missiles. The two

Invincible leaves Malta on 2 January 1995.
(Michael Cassar)

On 2 January 1995 *Invincible* is waved off by sightseers at Lower Barracca Gardens, Malta.
(Michael Cassar)

Invincible sails into a grey Mediterranean Sea on 2 January 1995, after having spent Christmas and New Year in Grand Harbour. *(Michael Cassar)*

around the city. Operating in conjunction with the US Navy's aircraft carriers *America* and *Roosevelt,* and with aircraft from Italian bases, the Sea Harriers undertook 24 bombing sorties, 42 combat air patrols and 28 reconnaissance missions during the ten-day campaign which was designed to force Serb compliance with United Nations Resolutions. At the end of the campaign the desired result was achieved when Bosnian Serb forces withdrew their heavy weapons from around the city of Sarajevo. The commanding officer of the Combined Air Operations Centre in Italy, who had controlled the air offensive, praised *Invincible's* contribution, as well as the expertise of the Sea Harrier pilots in using the aircraft's multi-role capability to such good effect, including accurate bombing, reliable air cover and effective reconnaissance patrols to assess bomb damage. He also made special mention of the 100 per cent serviceability rate of the FA2 Sea Harriers. Meanwhile, *Invincible's* commanding officer, Captain Ian Forbes, praised the professionalism of the

whole ship's company. As for the pilots, they found the new FA2 Sea Harrier to be a great improvement on the old FRS1, as one commented: 'It has a far better radar that can see much more and gives me a nice warm feeling, especially as I now have a good overall picture of where aircraft are. The risk of a blue-on-blue (a friendly fire incident) arising, or even a mid-air collision, is greatly reduced.' During the deployment *Invincible* also took part in 'Exercise Infinite Courage' with HMS *Cardiff,* USS *America,* RFA *Olwen* and other units. On 9 December 1995, having been relieved by *Illustrious, Invincible* arrived in Portsmouth to an enthusiastic greeting from families and friends. During the deployment she had remained at sea for over three-quarters of her time in the Mediterranean, conducting flying operations in support of the two NATO operations, 'Deny Flight' and 'Deliberate Force'. Her commanding officer received the Queen's Commendation for Valuable Service and the commanding officer of 800 Squadron was awarded an MBE. Later, for their role in the peace

A Sea Harrier flies over *Invincible* during her May 1995 deployment to the Adriatic.

(Official, Courtesy Derek Fox)

Invincible arrives at Portsmouth on 17 February 1996.

(Mike Lennon)

enforcement operations in Bosnia, *Invincible* and *Illustrious* were jointly awarded the Wilkinson Sword of Peace.

The early weeks of 1996 saw *Invincible* undergoing maintenance in Portsmouth Dockyard and when she put to sea, although still on standby for service in the Adriatic, with a peace agreement having been signed between the warring parties in the former Yugoslavia, her immediate presence in the area was not required. On 15 March, whilst in Portsmouth Dockyard, the ship received a visit from the Duke of York who launched the 'Swordfish Heritage Trust Appeal' on board. By June 1996 NATO's presence in the Adriatic was being scaled down and *Invincible's* initial sea time was spent in home waters, with a visit to Amsterdam. During a busy summer *Invincible* undertook successful trials operating RAF GR7 ground-attack aircraft. The trials, code-named 'Operation Hornpipe', were conducted by the Strike Attack Operational Evaluation Unit, and initial tests concentrated on ensuring that the aircraft's navigational systems were capable of alignment at sea. Once this had been proved, the trials were extended to include night launches and recoveries using the GR7's

electro-optical sensors. Although the RAF's ground attack Harriers had flown from *Invincible* during the Falklands War, these trials envisaged the regular deployment of whole units for weeks at a time, with ground crews accompanying the aircraft to sea. The ship also played a leading role in a Joint Maritime Course off Scotland and in Staff College Sea Days in the Channel, during which she operated with *Battleaxe, Manchester* and *Iron Duke.* For the JMC *Invincible* embarked the Deputy Flag Officer Surface Flotilla and his staff, and the exercises involved some 40 vessels and 150 aircraft from nine countries The carrier undertook live firings of her Sea Dart missiles, which all found their targets, and in late June the ship berthed at North Shields where, on open days, thousands of people queued to get on board. Renewing links to her affiliated city, the Mayor of Durham took passage up the River Tyne and later hosted a civic dinner and luncheon for officers and ratings. During Staff College Sea Days, wearing the flag of FO Surface Flotilla, *Invincible* returned to her flagship role and there were gunnery demonstrations by *Iron Duke* and *Manchester,* light jackstay transfers and aerial

During the forenoon of 19 December 1996, *Invincible* arrives back into a dull and grey Portsmouth Harbour after her deployment to the Persian Gulf and Mediterranean. *(Neil McCart)*

Invincible at Gareloch, 9 June 1997.   *(Brian Hargreaves)*

displays by Sea Kings, Sea Harriers and RAF Harriers. Among the VIPs welcomed on board was the C-in-C of the Chinese Navy, Admiral Lianzhang. There was also time to fit in the first Families Day for three years when, off the Nab Tower with *Glasgow* and *Manchester,* families and friends of the ship's company were treated to a flying display by Lynx and Sea King helicopters, and Sea Harriers. The climax of the day was a fly-past by a Fairey Swordfish from the Royal Navy's Historic Flight.

With summer leave over *Invincible* joined some 55 other warships from 11 nations off the coast of Norway for the NATO exercise 'Northern Lights'. The main object of this exercise was to ensure the safety of sea lanes through the Skagerrak in a hostile environment, with the multi-national force supported by submarines, auxiliaries and shore-based aircraft. *Invincible's* group consisted of HMS *Birmingham,* USS *Thorn,* ITS *Mimbelli,* SNS *Andalucia* and USS *Nicholson,* backed up by Danish and Norwegian fast patrol boats. Despite some severe weather the exercise proved an ideal opportunity for the integration of joint operations, and for *Invincible* it was her first opportunity to operate in northern waters following her tours of duty in the Adriatic. The exercise was followed by a passage to the

Mediterranean and 'Exercise Dynamic Mix', for which she flew the flag of the FO Surface Flotilla, Vice-Admiral J. Brigstocke. Nine nations had provided 30 ships and submarines for the two-week NATO programme which also involved HM Ships *Nottingham* and *Sheffield.* For the first time in three years three European aircraft carriers, *Invincible, Principe de Asturias* and *Garibaldi,* operated together and after rendezvousing at Palma, Majorca, they sailed for combined training, including air patrols, cross-deck exchanges and mixed fighter operations. *Invincible's* Sea Harriers also had the opportunity to conduct the first tests of new 540lb bombs on a southern Italian bombing range. The exercise featured some 17 engagements in one week, with the 'enemy' being provided by French, Italian and US units, while *Invincible's* Sea Kings provided the spotting capability. During her Mediterranean sojourn *Invincible* visited Palma, Piraeus and Izmir, before sailing south to pass through the Suez Canal and on to the Persian Gulf, where she was the first British aircraft carrier to visit the area for three years.

On arrival in the Persian Gulf *Invincible* and her escort *Sheffield* joined the units of the Armilla Patrol and an American battle group led by the carrier USS *Enterprise* for

An aerial view of *Invincible* during operations in the Persian Gulf during February 1998.

During the forenoon of 26 March 1998 *Invincible* returned to Portsmouth from the Persian Gulf.　　　　(Neil McCart)

Gulfex 96', a major joint tactical operation concentrating on surface and air warfare. Earlier in the year diplomatic tensions in the region had been high and *Invincible's* presence demonstrated Britain's military commitment to the Gulf area. It was the first time that a British carrier group had taken part in operational training in the Persian Gulf since the 1960s, and the opportunity was taken for *Invincible* to visit Dubai, Kuwait and Al Jubayl in Saudi Arabia. Operating in temperatures which frequently exceeded 38 degrees centigrade it was an ideal opportunity to prepare the squadrons and the ship's company for extreme weather conditions. At the end of the deployment *Invincible* returned to Portsmouth during the forenoon of Thursday 19 December 1996, just in time for Christmas.

Autumn 1996 marked the fourth anniversary of the first members of the Wrens being sent to sea, as an experiment, on board *Invincible*. Four years on and 110 members of her complement were female and, whether working in blue overalls on the lower deck, or wearing the starched white shirts of the wardroom, they were an integral part of the ship's company. Despite much criticism when they first joined the ship, by late 1996 the principle of mixed crews was no longer an issue and the ship functioned as efficiently as ever. During the forenoon of 9

January 1997, whilst *Invincible* lay at Portsmouth undergoing maintenance, she received a visit from the Prince of Wales who formally presented the ship with the 'Wilkinson Sword of Peace', which she had been awarded jointly with *Illustrious* for their contribution to the restoration of order in the former Yugoslavia. *Invincible* remained in home waters on completion of her maintenance period and over two weeks in June she led Joint Maritime Course 972 off the northern and western Scottish coasts. At one stage, negotiating the restricted waters of the Gare Loch, she became the first operational aircraft carrier to berth alongside at the Faslane Naval Base. During JMC 972, which involved forces from ten nations and included 23 warships and 92 military aircraft, *Invincible* played her part in a series of air defence, anti-submarine and mine-hunting exercises. In July, again wearing the flag of Vice-Admiral Brigstocke, the carrier led a task group of seven ships, including *Edinburgh, Iron Duke,* the Dutch frigate *Van Amstel* and the RFAs *Olwen* and *Sea Crusader,* for Staff College Sea Days. Officers from many countries and from all three services study at the college, and over several days they were given a series of power demonstrations off the Isle of Wight. Also attending were many top British businessmen, government officials and Members of Parliament, all eager to sample life at sea with the Royal Navy and to witness the flexibility which aircraft carriers bring to British defence capabilities. During the demonstrations *Invincible* was joined by FA2 Sea Harriers and RAF GR7 Harriers for practice bombing runs. During the same period, on a 'Royal Navy in the Public Eye' day, *Invincible* embarked over 100 VIPs, including the popular comedian Jimmy Tarbuck and the television personality Ned Sherrin, who also experienced life on board as they visited every department in the ship. During August, another VIP visitor was the Prince of Wales who spent a day at sea watching live firings and air displays, and meeting members of the ship's company.

On 2 September 1997 *Invincible* left Portsmouth to embark her air group, which consisted of the FA2 Sea Harriers of 800 Squadron and, for the first time on a routine operational cruise, five of the RAF's GR7 Harriers belonging to No 1 (Fighter) Squadron, based at RAF Wittering. She also embarked the AEW Sea Kings of 849A Flight and two ASW Sea Kings of 814 Squadron. However, with no room to spare for any more of the latter, the remaining aircraft were deployed to RFA *Fort Victoria*. After some years of trials from aircraft carriers, including *Invincible,* the RAF's Harriers were taking part in the first integrated FA2/GR7 operational exercise, which was code-named 'Tapon'. The 'tailored' air group was the most powerful deployment of air power at sea since the Falklands War and the exercise provided some challenging training for both air and deck crews. On board *Invincible* as she left Portsmouth was the Ukrainian Ambassador to London, whose day visit to the ship was part of the MoD's bilateral exercise programme with the former Soviet state. 'Exercise Tapon' was a major NATO multi-national training programme off southern Spain during which *Invincible* operated closely with her old 'friend' SNS *Principe de Asturias* and her complement of AV8B (Harrier) aircraft. At one stage a world 'first' was claimed by *Invincible* when she

carried out a combined launch of three Harrier variants. There were also simultaneous launches and recoveries of ten jets by day and eight by night, and it was clear that with the RAF capability of operating from aircraft carriers well and truly proven, a new era in Royal Navy aircraft carrier operations had arrived.

The exercise ended in late September and while *Invincible* was still off the southern Spanish coast the RAF Harriers returned to their UK base, with three of 800 Squadron's aircraft being launched to make an epic flight of some 4,500 miles to the west coast of America for further training. *Invincible* herself also set course for the United States, with her destination being the eastern seaboard for joint exercises with US forces. After visiting Norfolk, Virginia, the ship took part in combined flying operations with the US Marine Corps and Air Force, and all seemed to be set for further manoeuvres, a ten-day maintenance period at Mayport, Florida, where a number of wives and families had arranged to meet the ship, as well as visits to Caribbean ports before the ship returned via Barcelona where she would promote British trade, to Portsmouth in time for Christmas. However, it was not to be for in the Middle East a crisis had arisen over the issue of United Nations weapons inspectors and their free access to sites in Iraq. Although falling short of ordering a full-scale military attack on Iraq, the USA and Britain began a rapid build-up of their forces in the Persian Gulf in order to provide an overwhelming show of force in the area. Initially Britain's aerial contribution was to be RAF Tornado aircraft, but when it became clear that they would be denied the use of bases in Turkey and Saudi Arabia for any attack on Iraq, *Invincible* was ordered to sail with all dispatch for Gibraltar and prepare for service, and possible war, in the Persian Gulf. At the time the carrier was visiting Barbados before heading for her maintenance period at Mayport, but soon she was making a high-speed transatlantic dash to Gibraltar.

Chapter Seven

Into the 21st Century
November 1998 – August 2004

After making her fast transatlantic dash from the Caribbean *Invincible* arrived off Cape St Vincent on 19 November 1997, where she rendezvoused with *Illustrious* in order to embark additional personnel and equipment for her air group, as well as the Commander UK Task Group, Rear-Admiral Ian Forbes, before putting into Gibraltar later that day. There then followed a hectic 24 hours as she took on board her old friends from the RAF's No 1(F) Squadron, together with tons of stores which kept everyone busy for the whole night. Finally during the evening of 20 November, *Invincible* sailed east into the Mediterranean and the following afternoon she embarked seven RAF GR7 Harriers, which had flown out directly from their base at RAF Wittering.

With the arrival of the RAF's seven aircraft *Invincible* was once again fully laden with, by the standards of her class, a large carrier air group which consisted of eight FA2 Sea Harriers belonging to 800 Squadron, the seven RAF GR7s, four Sea King AEW helicopters of 849A Flight and two Sea King ASW helicopters of 814 Squadron. The remaining five of 814 Squadron's Sea Kings were deployed to RFA *Fort Victoria*. As soon as all the aircraft were on board *Invincible* began her work-up in earnest, assisted by the aircraft of the Fleet Requirement and Direction Unit and the availability of the Italian Air Force bombing range on the island of Sardinia. On 24 November the Secretary of State for Defence visited *Invincible* to announce: 'We cannot drop our guard until Saddam Hussein complies with the United Nations. *Invincible* and her air group remain a sensible option.' On the diplomatic front, although the Iraqis were still refusing access to a number of installations, it was apparent that they were giving ground. It was also clear that the USA and Britain had little world support for any full-scale invasion of Iraq, in what was seen by many to be a thinly disguised attempt by America to gain control of Iraq's rich oil reserves. Next day, during night flying operations off Sardinia, one of the RAF Harriers was lost. The aircraft, returning from a training mission, had begun the normal hovering manoeuvre on *Invincible's* port side before flying sideways to touch down on the flight deck when it crashed into the sea. With the help of two empty external fuel tanks the Harrier remained afloat, which enabled the pilot to escape and he was quickly rescued by the SAR helicopter. Within minutes,

with the ship having stopped, the crash boat with ship's divers on board was launched and the divers succeeded in placing two flotation bags underneath the stricken aircraft, keeping it on the surface. This allowed lifting strops to be placed under the fuselage, and it was lifted onto the flight deck where it was hosed down with fresh water.

As the 'crisis' in the Persian Gulf simmered on, *Invincible* continued her work-up. There was a short break at Barcelona where the scheduled change of commanding officers took place, before the ship sailed to the Adriatic to fulfil a planned commitment to 'Operation Deliberate Guard'. During the period off the former Yugoslavia some 53 sorties were flown over that troubled region of Europe before the carrier sailed west to Gibraltar where she arrived on 12 December. Four days before arriving in the colony, however, *Invincible* went to the aid of the Beirut-registered cargo ship *Megane* which in severe gales had shipped water, shed her deck cargo of timber, and was listing heavily. Two Sea Kings of 814 Squadron lifted six crewmen to safety, with the remaining seven being rescued by an Italian search and rescue helicopter. All the crewmen were transferred to *Invincible* for medical checks before being landed at Sicily. At this stage the optimists on board the carrier were still hopeful of getting home for Christmas, but their hopes were soon dashed when it was learned that *Invincible* would sail to the eastern Mediterranean and remain at short notice for a southbound passage through the Suez Canal. For the carrier's ship's company Christmas was spent at anchor off Akrotiri and, having been stood down for a short period, the New Year was seen in at Palermo. On 4 January 1998, however, *Invincible* was back at sea and carrying out another Adriatic patrol, when she and RFA *Fort Victoria* were ordered to proceed to the Persian Gulf. *Invincible* was to spearhead Britain's maritime force in the Persian Gulf in an operation code-named 'Operation Bolton', which was primarily a political and diplomatic campaign, backed up by the very real threat of force should Iraq fail to allow United Nations weapons inspectors access to suspected weapons sites. Given the possibility that the negotiations might fail, *Invincible* had to be prepared to conduct offensive action against specified targets in Iraq.

Invincible and *Fort Victoria* made their southbound transit of the Suez Canal on 18 January 1998, and coinciding with this *Illustrious* left Portsmouth bound for

Invincible entering the River Tyne on 25 July 2000.

(Brian Hargreaves)

Invincible leaves Portsmouth on 15 January 2001 for exercises in northern waters. *(Derek Fox)*

the Mediterranean where she would carry out her work-up, before proceeding to the Persian Gulf where she was due to relieve *Invincible.* Meanwhile, having made her way south through the Red Sea, *Invincible* was exercising in the Gulf of Aden when one of her Sea Harriers on a training mission some 70 miles from the ship lost its canopy at 40,000 feet. Within seconds, despite the sudden decompression and the tremendous wind forces pulling at everything in the cockpit, the pilot managed to plummet 37,000 feet then, without any communications, he flew the aircraft back to the ship. He was subsequently awarded the Queen's Commendation for Bravery. On 25 January *Invincible* passed through the Strait of Hormuz and whilst in the Gulf *Invincible's* aircraft patrolled the southern 'No-Fly Zone' over Iraq, and joined American carrier-borne aircraft on bombing training in the area. The ship herself, as well as joining forces with *Coventry* and *Nottingham,* operated in conjunction with a powerful US Navy carrier group and at one stage, when it appeared that political negotiations were about to break down, *Invincible's* aircraft were at 24-hours' notice to launch bombing attacks against Iraqi targets. On board *Invincible,* with action coveralls having been issued,

with battle bags being carried and the ship secured for action, conditions on board were tense. There was, however, a 'determined professionalism' on board as it became apparent that events appeared to be moving inexorably towards some sort of conflict. As the political negotiations reached a crucial stage, all eyes were glued to the live satellite television reports in the wardroom and on all the mess decks. In the event a last-minute intervention by the United Nations defused the crisis and provided a solution which was satisfactory to all parties. *Invincible* made visits to Dubai and Bahrain but, to the relief of all on board, on 1 March *Illustrious* took over responsibility for heading the British military presence in the area and, as the United Nations Security Council endorsed the peace deal with Iraq, *Invincible* began her long journey home. Finally, during the forenoon of Thursday 26 March, in lashing rain and driving winds, *Invincible* returned to Portsmouth. Needless to say the inclement weather did nothing to dampen the enthusiasm of the ship's company and the families who were there to greet them.

Following her extended deployment to the Persian Gulf *Invincible* underwent a maintenance period at Portsmouth

(Courtesy Derek Fox)

In the Norwegian Fjords in the early weeks of 2001. She is wearing the Combined Operations funnel badge.

Dockyard, with most of the work being undertaken by Fleet Support Ltd, the new company managing the dockyard's maintenance and repair organization. Following her return to sea in the summer of 1998 *Invincible* became the first Royal Navy aircraft carrier since the early 1970s to enter the Baltic Sea, and her four-day visit to the Polish port of Gdynia, from 25 to 29 July, was definitely a special occasion. Flying the flag of Rear-Admiral P. Franklyn, *Invincible's* visit coincided with the 80th anniversary celebrations of the formation of the Polish Navy, and prior to the break-up of the Soviet-led Eastern Bloc such a visit by a Royal Navy aircraft carrier would have been unthinkable. During *Invincible's* stay the former Polish President Lech Walesa was one of the VIP guests welcomed on board and, with his wife and children, he was given a guided tour of the ship by the ship's commanding officer. The carrier's visit also coincided with high-level talks on Poland's proposed entry into NATO. Such was the local interest in the Royal Navy, that when *Invincible* was opened to the public some 11,000 visitors queued to get aboard. Ashore, meanwhile, the Sea Harriers took part in an airshow at a nearby base, and the embarked Royal Marines Band gave concerts at Gdansk, Sopot and Gdynia. *

That summer, during the public holiday period, *Invincible* was the main attraction at Portsmouth's International Festival of the Sea, and this was followed by Sea Days off the Isle of Wight. In company with the destroyer *Liverpool,* the frigates *Brave* and *Richmond,* the minehunters *Hurworth* and *Walney* and two support vessels, the exercises saw *Invincible* put on a series of manoeuvres and displays to teachers and industrialists which were designed to attract recruits to the service. In October there was a visit to Liverpool, and one of the carrier's helicopters went to the aid of the trawler *Amber Rose* which had sunk in the Irish Sea, south of the Isle of Man. In the event five crewmen were rescued by the RAF, but the vessel's skipper was lost. *Invincible* remained in home waters during November, and in December she returned to Portsmouth for maintenance and leave. It was during the leave period that political events in the Middle East once again affected *Invincible's* programme, and during the forenoon of Saturday 9 January 1999, together with the destroyer *Newcastle,* the carrier left for the Persian Gulf. Next day, in the Channel, she embarked the Sea Harriers of 800 Squadron and not long afterwards one of her helicopters went to the aid of a cargo ship, taking off a sick crewman for medical treatment at a French hospital. As well as *Invincible* and *Newcastle* the RFAs *Bayleaf* and *Fort Austin* formed part of the group, but this time the carrier did not have the RAF's GR7 Harriers on board. The passage to the Persian Gulf was made with only one stop

off the coast of Cyprus where stores were replenished, and on 21 January she passed through the Suez Canal. Eight days later the group passed through the Strait of Hormuz and into the operational area, where they joined *Cumberland* and *Boxer* which were already operating the Armilla Patrol. Within 24 hours of her arrival *Invincible's* Sea Harriers were operating with US aircraft in 'Operation Southern Watch', the enforcement of the No-Fly Zone over Iraq. Because of the limited flying range of the Sea Harriers *Invincible* operated well to the north of the Persian Gulf, and within range of any possible Iraqi air strike, so the role of the escorts *Cumberland* and *Newcastle* was crucial.

On 1 April 1999, in accordance with the scheduled plans, *Invincible* and *Newcastle* left the Persian Gulf to make her passage home, but nine days later they were ordered to sail for the Ionian Sea to provide military support for 'Operation Allied Force', the NATO bombing of Serb military and strategic targets in Kosovo, including bridges, roads, ammunition and fuel stores and radio communications. Once again the carrier's homecoming would be delayed, but *Inivincible's* presence strengthened the British contribution to the Balkan peacekeeping operations, and after a rapid transit of the Suez Canal and resupply at Cyprus, she arrived on station on 14 April. Two days later the Sea Harriers made their first operational missions, which they continued throughout the ship's stay in the area, mainly covering airfields at Pristina and Podgorica. On 21 May, with sufficient NATO aircraft in the area, *Invincible* and *Newcastle* were withdrawn from the UK Task Group and six days later they arrived home in Portsmouth to a rapturous welcome from families and friends.

Soon after her return to Portsmouth *Invincible* began a major overhaul during which, at the expense of her Sea Dart anti-aircraft missile launcher in the bow of the ship, she was fitted with extra flight deck space for the RAF's GR7 Harriers. Her main propulsion machinery received a thorough overhaul and as she sat in dry dock she looked more like a building site with scaffolding obscuring her superstructure. Below decks loose wiring hung from deckheads, deck coverings were torn up and her flight deck was littered with huts, tools and equipment, which gave the appearance of a desolate wasteland. Her complement was reduced to around 400, and they were joined by over 300 members of the dockyard's Fleet Support Ltd staff. The cost of the overhaul was around £24 million, with the main objective being to enhance the ship's ability to operate the FA2 Sea Harriers, the RAF's GR7 Harriers and, to a limited extent, the Fleet Air Arm's new Merlin helicopters. Finally, after seven months in dockyard hands, during the spring of 2000 the carrier was set to return to sea.

* In its modern form Poland came about as a result of the First World War. Its borders, drawn up at Versailles, were always a source of controversy and Gdansk was formerly the German city of Danzig.

Another view of *Invincible* in the Norwegian Fjords.

(*Derek Fox*)

On 25 July 2001 *Invincible* arrived at Rosyth to begin a £65 million refit which would keep her out of service until early 2003. *(Dave Cullen)*

During her post-refit trials *Invincible* operated in her LPH role, and here she is wearing the 'Combined Operations' funnel badge.

(*Dave Cullen*)

On 3 March 2000, for the first time since May the previous year, *Invincible* left Portsmouth and put to sea to begin what would be three months of intensive sea trials. During the course of the trials it was learned that *Invincible* would be paid off for the last time before the first of two proposed new 40,000-ton aircraft carriers, which were due for completion in 2012, came into service. Although no specific date was given it was an acknowledgement that *Invincible* was one of the Royal Navy's 'old ladies'. The news did not, however, alter the fact that the refit had brought the 'old lady' into the 21st century and to the position where, in the words of her commanding officer, '*Invincible* can match punch for punch any other carrier. Now we can land, re-arm and reload 16 aircraft much more quickly which makes us more effective. In the past we were making do with facilities. Now they are tailor made.' Soon after her return to sea following her own massive package of maintenance work, *Invincible*'s engineers were able to go to the aid of a small fishing craft, *Scooby Doo*, and carry out the much more modest task of repairing the boat's outboard motor which had broken down and left her

drifting helplessly. With the rescue mission completed the carrier was able to continue her trials and training programme, and during May she underwent three weeks of intensive activity under the watchful eye of the Flag Officer Sea Training's staff. In July, with her trials and tribulations over, she took over front-line duties from *Illustrious* and prepared for a six-week public relations and recruiting programme. Between 27 May and mid-July a 24-ship Royal Navy task group toured British ports on a 'Meet the Navy' millennium tour with *Invincible* joining in on 17 June at Greenock. Accompanied by HMS *Liverpool*, this was followed on 24 June with two days in the River Mersey at Liverpool and on 30 June *Invincible* sailed up the Bristol Channel to the Royal Portbury Docks near Bristol where, over just two days, she received over 5,000 visitors. The high-profile event saw all the Bristol Channel ports receive visits from HM Ships, with *Raider* and *Tracker* negotiating the Sharpness Canal to call at Gloucester, while HMS *Smiter* sailed up the Avon into the centre of Bristol. *Somerset* and *Quorn* secured alongside at Avonmouth, *Exeter* and *Penzance* at Swansea and *Chiddingfold* at

With her last long refit over and snow covering the flight deck, *Invincible* leaves Rosyth on 15 February 2003 to carry out post-refit trials.   (*Dave Cullen*)

Cardiff. *Invincible's* final visit on 7 July took her up the River Thames, through the Thames Barrier to berth in the Pool of London at Greenwich. On 13 July Her Majesty the Queen visited *Invincible* where she was received on board by the commanding officer, and entertained to lunch in the wardroom.

On completion of her recruiting tour *Invincible* sailed north for Scottish waters where she took part in JMC 002. Originally she had been scheduled to cross the Atlantic for the eastern seaboard of the United States, but events in the Balkans were to dictate *Invincible's* movements once again; Serbian forces were thought to be planning a military operation in Montenegro to coincide with presidential elections, and so it was decided to keep *Invincible* in readiness for duty in the Adriatic. On 4 September 2000, with summer leave having been taken, *Invincible* left Portsmouth with RFA *Fort George* and sailed for the eastern Mediterranean. Embarked for the deployment were the Sea Harriers of 800 Squadron, the GR7 Harriers of the RAF's 1(F) Squadron and the Sea Kings of 814 and 849 Squadrons. They were joined en route by the destroyer *Liverpool*, and after leaving Gibraltar they took part in Mediterranean exercises. During one such exercise a distress call was received from the yacht *Kabuki*, which had lost her sail and was taking in water off the Algerian coast. *Invincible* was some 15 miles away at the time and she immediately launched a rescue helicopter. Just over 15 minutes after receiving the call the helicopter was over the scene where it rescued the yacht's two crew members from the sea and flew them back to the ship for medical attention, as well as dry clothes and hot coffee. Later in September, as presidential elections got under way in the rump state of Yugoslavia and political tensions mounted, *Invincible*, *Ocean* and *Liverpool* reinforced the NATO armada at the edge of the Adriatic in a show of strength designed to send a message to Slobodon Milosovic not to try to cling to power if defeated at the ballot box.

Meanwhile, during the afternoon of Tuesday 26 September, as *Invincible* was some 50 miles south of the Greek island of Paros, the aged Greek ferry *Express Samina* pulled out of Piraeus Harbour bound for Paros, Naxos, Samos, Ikaria, Patros and Lipsi, just as she had on thousands of occasions during her 15-year career plying the seas around the Greek islands. On board she had over 530 passengers and her first port of call was Paros, which should have been a five-hour journey. However, since mid-afternoon strong winds had been blowing and by the time she sailed, Force 8 gales were whipping up dense streaks of foam as angry waves toppled and tumbled and reduced visibility even further on what was a dark and stormy night. Many passengers later reported that more than just a few crew members were packed with passengers in the lounges watching an international football match on television. Suddenly, at 22.20, as passengers looked outside

they were horrified to see that the ferry's starboard side was virtually alongside a huge 80-foot high rock. Within seconds there was a loud, jolting crash and the ferry took a violent list to starboard. *Express Samina* had hit Portes Reef, which was both well charted and marked with a lighthouse, some three miles from Paros, and she immediately began to sink. On board the ferry, with no power and with no leadership on board, there was chaos as both passengers and crew scrambled for life jackets and life-rafts. Others, unable to find life jackets, stampeded for the stern as the stricken ferry began sinking by the bow.

As the passengers on board *Express Samina* desperately tried to save themselves, less than 60 miles away *Invincible*, *Liverpool* and RFA *Fort George* were engaged in exercises, which for *Invincible* included a fixed- and rotary-wing day and night flying programme, when a distress message was received on board. Within minutes, on a particularly dark night with no visual horizon, with strong winds of 30 to 40 knots blowing and a heavy sea, helicopters were on their way to the wreck site. The duty search and rescue from 814 Squadron, Lieutenants Gary Milton, Al Hinchcliffe and Tim Hayden, together with crewman LACMN Nicholas Hipkin, arrived to find survivors who had been thrown from a lifeboat clinging to a low-lying rock that was being constantly battered by the gale force winds and huge waves. The proximity of the rock to the high ground of the treacherous and unfamiliar cliffs made the task of positioning the aircraft extremely difficult and required the absolute attention and direction of all four crew members. With only limited visual references to guide him, Lt Hinchcliffe maintained his position for 45 minutes, while in the rear of the helicopter Lt Milton and LACMN Hipkin, with little regard for their own safety, battled with appalling conditions to rescue all 12 people who were stranded on the rock. Once the last person was inside the helicopter it returned to *Invincible* where the survivors were handed over to medical teams. Lt Gary Milton later described events: 'After nearly an hour of flying we were less than 100 yards from the cliffs when we spotted a small ship that was illuminating the survivors. The rock was four metres square and one metre high. The tide was rising and the sea-state meant that the waves were repeatedly breaking over their heads. The heavy sea spray and poor visibility was so bad that we couldn't initially assess how many people there were. A difficult hover was established and LACMN Hipkin was lowered down for the first transfer. Once there he battled against the crashing waves and quickly calmed down the panicking survivors. He prioritized the order in which people had to be winched and we began the arduous task of bringing survivors to the aircraft. During two of the lifts he was swept off the rocks but he continued with the recovery. As each survivor was brought to the aircraft they were suffering from cuts and bruises and varying degrees of shock. A couple were

Arriving at Portsmouth on 14 March 2003 from her long refit at Rosyth.

(Derek Fox)

Invincible and *Ark Royal* (nearest) alongside at Portsmouth during August 2003.

(*Neil McCart*)

Invincible leaves Portsmouth on 16 October 2003 for exercises in the North Sea.

(James W. Goss)

Eight RAF GR7 Harriers of No 3(F) Squadron undertake a fly-past of *Invincible* before…

…Landing on board for the first time. *(Neil McCart)*

Sea Harriers landing on during North Sea exercises in October 2003.

(PO PHOT Paul Smith, HMS Invincible)

Launch of a Sea Harrier, October 2003.

(PO PHOT Paul Smith, HMS Invincible)

suffering from hypothermia and another man had an injured leg. Time was running out so I decided to recover all 12 from the rocks to the aircraft in one go, even though this was more than a Sea King Mk 6 would normally carry. By the time all the survivors had been winched on board, *Invincible* was 18 miles away and closing at 25 knots. The pilot had to land on No 3 spot and the darkness, marginal weather and high nose-up attitude of the helicopter made it very difficult.' In the event some 80 people lost their lives in the disaster, with the other survivors being rescued by the dozen passenger ferries and 40 fishing vessels which had gathered at the scene.

During her Mediterranean deployment, although *Invincible* did not actually enter the Adriatic, her presence in the area helped to deter further problems in the Balkan states. As well as working with the giant US Navy carrier *George Washington* and carrying out air defence exercises, she visited Cyprus, Haifa, Majorca, Malaga and Malta. At Malaga she provided the venue for a BBC Television recording titled 'Homeward Bound for Christmas'. It had originally been intended to stage this on board HMS *Ocean,* but when she was redeployed to Sierra Leone *Invincible* stood in at the last minute and 'stole' the show. A touch of glamour was brought to the flight deck by the pop groups S Club 7 and Atomic Kitten, the singer and actress Martine McCutcheon and the presenter Melinda Messenger. Leading the entertainment group was the veteran comedian Jim Davidson, with his co-presenter Suzi Perry, and just as popular as the rest were the actor Sir John Mills and the Olympic rowers Steve Redgrave and Matthew Pinsent. Finally, after more training exercises and having covered a total of 9,000 miles, on Saturday 18 November *Invincible* returned to Portsmouth.

During December 2000, with 814 Squadron having been paid off and it having been announced that *Invincible* would remain in Portsmouth Harbour from April to July 2001, when she would sail north to Rosyth for a major refit, rumours about her impending demise began to circulate. These rumours were emphatically denied by the MoD who announced that she would be given one final major refit which would keep her in service for another 12 years. That winter, as the carrier lay in Portsmouth Dockyard, the ship's Engineering Department made a break with the past when the liquid oxygen plant was shut down for the last time. Ordinarily, with machinery being replaced and updated on a regular basis one might wonder what was special about the liquid oxygen plant, until one learned that it was a relic from the old fleet aircraft carrier HMS *Eagle,* into which it had been fitted in 1953. It had been removed from *Eagle* in the early 1970s and then fitted in *Invincible* when she was built. The plant was eventually removed during *Invincible's* major refit at Rosyth, and replaced with more modern equipment.

The new year of 2001 saw *Invincible* at sea in northern

waters and providing the venue for the research agency QinetiQ's vectored thrust aircraft which carried out trials as part of a research programme into the technologies required for 'Future Carrier Based Aircraft'. The specially built Harrier demonstrated the capability to fly automatically to a moving recovery point, in order that future aircraft could operate in much poorer weather conditions than is possible with Harriers, for which *Invincible* provided a realistic environment at sea. The early weeks of the year also saw *Invincible* taking part in her last major exercise before her extended refit at Rosyth, and this time she took on the LPH role, together with the troop-carrying Sea King Mk 4 helicopters of 845 and 846 Squadrons, as well as a Lynx and a Gazelle from 847 Squadron, and she even operated RAF Chinook helicopters. Also embarked were elements of 3 Commando Brigade, including men of 42 Commando, who had been in Norway for some weeks. *Invincible's* role in the exercises began after a visit to North Shields in early February, and it saw her sail north inside the Arctic Circle to the bitterly cold and glassy waters of the Norwegian fjords. Also embarked were the staff of Commodore Amphibious Task Group, who converted the Admiral's quarters into their operations room. Parts of the hangar and flight deck, meanwhile, were used as stowage areas for the marines' equipment. Working in overnight temperatures as low as minus 25 degrees Centigrade, conditions were very different from those encountered during the previous Mediterranean exercises, and there were added complications when the outbreak of 'foot and mouth' disease in Britain, which devastated the agricultural industry at home, restricted the movement of personnel and equipment in Norway. *Invincible* went alongside at Harstad to embark 42 Commando where, in temperatures of just 3 degrees Centigrade, the ship's divers had to clear tangled fishing nets from the ship's propellers and stabilizers. The restrictions placed on the ship meant that the Royal Marines carried out their 'landing' in Scotland rather than Norway, and a call at Lossiemouth enabled several hundred families of service personnel serving in the Middle East to embark as 'refugees' for a simulated 'non-combatant evacuation exercise'. The exercises ended at Rosyth in late March and after five days in the Firth of Forth *Invincible* returned to Portsmouth where, as *Illustrious* took on the role of front-line aircraft carrier, *Invincible* was reduced to a lower state of readiness. During her stay at Portsmouth *Invincible's* complement was reduced to approximately 200 and stores, ammunition and engineering equipment was disembarked. On 23 July 2001, with her Type 996 radar mast having been removed, she left Portsmouth to make the two-day passage to Rosyth to begin a £65 million refit which would keep her out of service until early 2003.

The factors that determined the work carried out

Flying operations on a busy flight deck.

Flying operations.

Invincible at Glen Mallon, Loch Long.　　　　　　　　　　　　*(MOD Crown Copyright)*

An RAF Chinook helicopter operates with *Invincible*.

(*MOD Crown Copyright*)

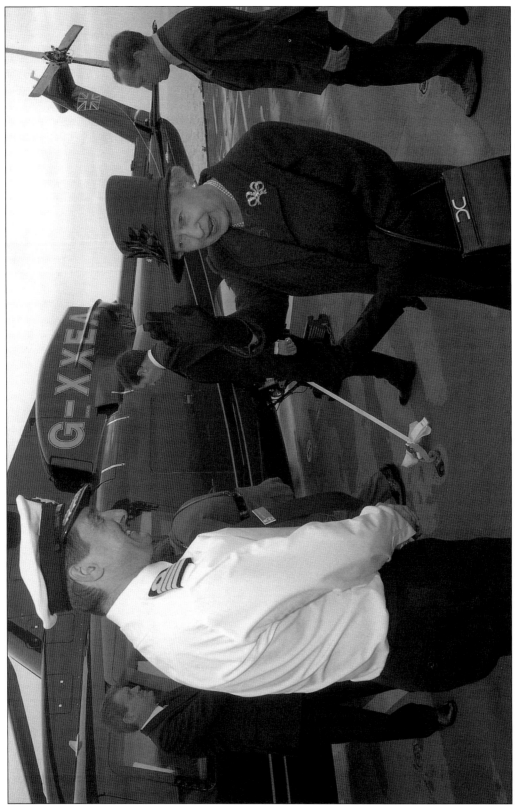

Her Majesty the Queen bids farewell to *Invincible*'s ship's company following her day at sea in the Channel on 27 April 2004. *(MOD Crown Copyright)*

during *Invincible's* Rosyth refit became clear when it was announced that in early 2006 the ship would be withdrawn from active service and placed in 'extended readiness' which, in reality, meant in Reserve. This was four years earlier than had originally been planned, so it was apparent that the carrier's long career was entering its final phase, with the refit being 'tailored' to prepare the ship for just two-and-a-half years of further operational service. During the refit *Invincible's* flight deck was strengthened to enable the ship to operate Merlin helicopters, the ship's IT systems were fully networked, the accommodation was refurbished and there was a complete overhaul of the main propulsion machinery. One major task was the removal and replacement of the massive starboard main gearwheel, which weighs some 20 tons and which was lifted from the vessel using lifting and jacking techniques which had been specially designed for the operation. The largest single task, however, was the updating and reconfiguration of the ship's main operations room. After a long period in dry dock, on 11 July 2002 *Invincible* was refloated and on 12 December that year the carrier's new commanding officer, Captain T. A. Soar OBE RN, joined the ship. It was not long afterwards, as the ship was prepared for sea again, that the ship's company was brought up to strength once more.

In early February 2003 *Invincible* left the security of Rosyth Dockyard to begin a programme of trials in and around the Firth of Forth. The Marine Engineering and Weapons Engineering Departments conducted their various tests on the engines, gearboxes, steering gear and the close-in weapons systems. Although there were no embarked squadrons on board, the flight deck was kept busy with visits from the RAF and civilian Sea King helicopters, the latter being used for the transfer of staff, a number of VIP visitors and stores. On completion of the trials *Invincible* returned to Rosyth for defect repairs and maintenance before, on Friday 14 March 2003, after an absence of almost two years, she returned to Portsmouth where she was greeted by families and friends who 'took over' the Round Tower at Old Portsmouth, and with a fly-past by a Sea Harrier.

On 28 April 2003, having carried out more trials in the Channel, *Invincible* left Portsmouth and set course for the River Mersey and Liverpool, where she acted as flagship for the 60th anniversary celebrations of the Battle of the Atlantic.* With *Invincible* being the focal point for the event the C-in-C Fleet, Admiral Sir Jonathon Band, took the opportunity to visit and tour the ship. From Liverpool *Invincible* sailed north for the Firth of Clyde and the Glen Mallon depot at Loch Long, where she embarked ammunition before returning to Portsmouth to prepare for her seven-week period of Operational Sea Training. Before this arduous period commenced, however, there was an enjoyable and much more informal Families Day, with 900 guests being entertained to a day at sea off the Isle of Wight. Phase One of sea training was spent in the South Coast Exercise Areas, south of Plymouth where, day and night, on-board fires, floods and battle damage incidents tested the ship's company. For the first time in two years the ship embarked her 'Tailored Air Group', which consisted of the FA2 Sea Harriers of 801 Squadron and the Sea Kings of 824 Squadron and 849B Flight. Phase Two of *Invincible's* OST was spent in the North Sea, operating east of the Firth of Forth and off the coast of Northumberland. This phase was marked by a significant increase in the intensity and complexity of flying serials, with realistic scenarios which saw 801 Squadron's Sea Harriers coming up against Dutch and US F16s, and RAF Jaguars, Hawks and Falcons. The whole period culminated in *Invincible's* Operational Readiness Inspection, at the end of which the Flag Officer Sea Training congratulated the ship's company for receiving such a high assessment. Fortunately, the arduous weeks of sea training were followed by some well-deserved leave.

In early September *Invincible* was at sea again and carrying out deck landing practice with the two-seater T8 Harriers of 899 Squadron, before taking part in the major NATO exercise code-named 'Northern Light'. Some 50 warships, fighter planes and 500 troops joined the 12-day exercise which was designed to showcase the maritime and amphibious capabilities of a new NATO response force, which included Ukrainian and Lithuanian forces. Embarked in *Invincible* was the UK Maritime Force HQ staff, and amphibious landings were carried out at Luce Bay near Stranraer during the weekend of 20/21 September. Finally, on 30 September, with the demanding nine-month trials and training period over, *Invincible* assumed the duties of the high-readiness Fleet Flagship. It was in this role that, in early October, the ship paid a four-day visit to Tenerife, where she secured alongside the quay at Santa Cruz and she hosted a number of diplomatic functions. On 10 October she arrived back in Portsmouth for a short break before leaving six days later to begin a six-week training period in northern waters. Leaving Portsmouth during the afternoon, no sooner had the Nab Tower faded into the distance than eight GR7 Harriers from the RAF's No 3(F) Squadron roared overhead as they made an impressive low-level fly-past of the ship before landing on board. Most of the pilots were making their first carrier landing and the event was celebrated appropriately in the wardroom that evening. During their training period on board seven GR7s, together with nine Sea Harriers from 800 and 801 Squadrons, were launched in the space of five minutes, which was believed to be the largest ever single launch from such an aircraft carrier. There were visits to

---

* Other warships attending included HM Ships *Biter, Charger* and *Walney;* BNS *Primula;* FS *La Touche-Treville;* FGS *Schleswig-Holstein;* HMNLS *Schiedam;* HNOMS *Trondheim;* ORP *Kaszub* and RFS *Admiral Chabanyenko.*

North Shields and Rosyth, but with pressure on to complete the training programme, a proposed visit to Hamburg was cancelled. In the last week of November *Invincible* returned to Portsmouth, six days ahead of schedule, for some serious cleaning and painting in order to prepare the ship for her rededication ceremony.

For what was clearly going to be the carrier's last rededication, Her Majesty the Queen, who had launched the ship in her Jubilee Year of 1977, and who had been the guest of honour at the commissioning and recommissioning ceremonies in 1980 and 1989 respectively, was once again going to visit 'her' ship. The date had been set for Friday 12 December, but three days before the ceremony it was learned that the Queen had to undergo a knee operation and would be unable to attend, which was a great disappointment to all on board. At short notice the Duke of York, HRH Prince Andrew, stood in for his mother which, as an ex-*Invincible* himself, was very appropriate. Among the 2,000 invited guests, as well as families and friends of ship's company members, were the First Sea Lord, the C-in-C Fleet, and ten of the 12 former commanding officers of *Invincible*. The cake was cut by the youngest serving crew member, Steward S. Dawson, and by Mrs Anne Soar, the commanding officer's wife. As well as giving the nervous steward advice on how to cut through the generous layer of icing, the Duke of York also dispensed with a great deal of formality when he met serving members of the ship's company and their families. For *Invincible* it was the start of the last chapter of her long career.

In February 2004, prior to setting sail for exercises off Norway, the ship's company conducted an anti-terrorism 'Ship Protection Organization Exercise' whilst alongside in Portsmouth Harbour. This involved the ship's boat darting around the harbour at speeds of up to 25 knots, simulating a suicide attack as the ship's company on board practised 'eliminating' the 'terrorists' with machine-guns. It was a reminder of how the dangers facing Britain had changed during the 24 years that the ship had been in service with the Royal Navy. On 23 February, *Invincible* left Portsmouth to conduct training exercises off the south coast with 845 Squadron and elements of 3 Commando Brigade, before taking part in the appropriately named amphibious exercise 'Joint Winter 04', which comprised cold weather training in the Narvik area of Norway. Other units involved in the exercise included the new amphibious assault ship *Albion,* the destroyer *Manchester,* the frigate *Iron Duke* and RFAs *Sir Percivale, Sir Galahad, Sir Tristram, Fort George, Fort Rosalie* and *Brambleleaf.* In her role as a commando carrier *Invincible* operated with Sea King and Chinook helicopters which, in the words of her commanding officer, provided quite a contrast to just a few months earlier when, 'we were operating 18 Royal Navy and RAF Harrier aircraft from our deck.' During the

exercise there was an opportunity for the ship's company to experience a run ashore in the gloomy, snowbound town of Tromso and, on completion of the exercise, the far more hospitable city of Copenhagen. During the visit the ship was opened to the public, and although it had been thought that two hours would be long enough to get all interested visitors around, in the event almost 8,000 people turned up, so the gangway was kept open until the early evening. On 2 April, after some six weeks in Arctic waters, *Invincible* returned to Portsmouth.

Just over three weeks later, on 26 April, *Invincible* sailed for VIP Sea Days in the Channel. At 11.15 next day, in blustery weather off the Dorset coast, Her Majesty the Queen, travelling in a Sea King helicopter of the Royal Flight, landed on the carrier's flight deck, where she was met by the commanding officer and taken down to the aircraft hangar to meet assembled members of the ship's company before lunching with Captain Soar and a small cross-section of officers and members of the ship's company. During the afternoon the Queen's itinerary included a tour of the operations room and a visit to the Admiral's bridge to watch a flying demonstration by four Harriers and a Sea King, after which she left the ship in the Royal Flight helicopter. On 29 April there was a brief visit to Devonport, and next day *Invincible* returned to Portsmouth where there was a change of command and the ship was prepared for her next major deployment.

On 6 May 2004 *Invincible* left Portsmouth to lead 12 British warships, including *Albion, Ocean, Marlborough, Sutherland, Roebuck* and *Cornwall,* as well as four mine countermeasures vessels and their command ship RFA *Sir Bedivere,* on multi-national exercises which took place between the eastern seaboard of the USA and the Gulf of Mexico. 'Exercise Aurora' involved some 6,000 British service personnel, as well as units from the USA, Australia, Canada, Denmark, France, Germany, Holland, Italy, Norway and Peru. Embarked in *Invincible* were the Sea Harriers of 801 Squadron, together with the RAF's GR7 Harriers of No 3(F) Squadron. On board *Albion* and *Ocean* were the men of 42 Commando and 3 Commando Brigade and travelling with *Invincible* was the Royal Marines Band from Britannia Royal Naval College. As well as the exercises, the ships' companies of the Royal Navy units would enjoy runs ashore in the Azores, Bermuda, Florida, Virginia, Massachusetts, Nova Scotia, Newfoundland and New York.

With the Royal Navy's contingent making the transatlantic crossing in small groups at different times it was not until they reached Norfolk, Virginia, that they all rendezvoused for the main exercise, code-named 'Rapid Alliance', but this was not before *Invincible* had visited Mayport, Florida. During the Atlantic passage *Invincible's* ship's company had carried out some intensive exercises and, as the weather became warmer, there was a flight deck barbecue, with musical entertainment from the Royal Marines Band. An improvised Field Gun Competition was held, which involved pulling a five-ton flight deck tractor, and a 'Gala Concert' was staged in the hangar. After leaving the US naval base at Norfolk *Invincible* sailed for the exercise areas off the east coast of the USA, where she was joined by aircraft of 801 and 3(F) Squadrons who had been training on America's West Coast. For some personnel there was an opportunity to experience life aboard the giant Nimitz-class aircraft carrier USS *Theodore Roosevelt* before, on 12 June, 'Rapid Alliance' got under way. The exercise was a massive test of the amphibious capability of the Allied nations. For the Royal Navy it was the first big trial of its enhanced capability, with *Albion* and *Ocean* serving as the springboard for the main assault as troops were ferried ashore by helicopter and landing craft. Following the demise of the assault ships *Fearless* and *Intrepid,* with *Albion's* deployment came the reintroduction of the Navy's ability to land main battle tanks from the sea, and she actually deployed four of the Army's Challenger 2 tanks. Air cover for the landings was provided by *Invincible's* Sea Harriers and GR7s and among senior visitors to the exercises was the C-in-C Fleet, Admiral Sir Jonathon Band, who spent the day on board and met many members of the ship's company. On 1 July, with the exercises over, *Invincible, Cornwall* and RFA *St George* docked in New York for a six-day visit which took in the 4th July Independence Day celebrations. For the ships' companies it

was the highlight of the deployment, and it marked the culmination of successful exercises for the carrier and her task group. With the ship's company manning the flight and weather decks, *Invincible* sailed up the Hudson River to secure alongside New York's Pier 88, next to the main passenger terminal and the new Cunard cruise ship *Queen Mary 2,* on the western side of Manhattan Island. During her stay there were a number of high-profile events, including an official cocktail party which was attended by the British Ambassador to the United Nations, and the ship's previous commanding officer, Rear-Admiral Trevor Soar; the ringing of the Wall Street Stock Exchange bell by *Invincible's* commanding officer; an open-air concert by the Royal Marines Band in nearby Hanover Square in the heart of Lower Manhattan and the opening of the ship to visitors on 4 July. Two days later the visit came to an end and on 16 July *Invincible* returned to Portsmouth.

As *Invincible* completes the final months of her operational service, after 25 years of active service with the fleet, during which time both the British and Argentine Governments had planned her demise, today, in the uncertain post-Cold War era, she remains at the forefront of the country's defences. She and her squadrons have 'projected' British power in a dangerous and changing world, and she has paved the way for a new generation of aircraft carriers, the first of which, HMS *Queen Elizabeth,* should join the fleet in the second decade of the 21st century.

Appendix One
Principal Particulars

Deep Displacement:	19,810 tons
Length Overall:	206.3m/677ft
Beam:	35m/115ft
Draught:	26.5m/29ft
Armament:	One twin Sea Dart GWS30 sea-air missile launcher (removed 1999). Two Phalanx CIWS (added 1982). Four seven-barrelled 30mm Goalkeeper CWIS (added 1988).
Aircraft:	Up to 20. A 'tailored' mix of FA2 Sea Harriers, RAF GR7 Harriers, AEW and ASW Sea Kings/Merlin helicopters.
Hangar:	152.4m x 22.55m (500ft x 74ft)
Lifts:	16.6m x 9.6m (54ft - 6in x 31ft - 8in) forward and aft.
Main Propulsion Machinery:	Twin fixed-pitch, skew-bladed propellers, driven by four Rolls Royce Olympus TBM3 Gas Turbines, each with 170-ton reversing gearbox.
SHP:	112,000.
Speed:	28-30 knots (5,000 miles at 18 knots).
Complement:	686
With Embarked Squadrons:	1052.
Flight Deck:	167.6m x 19.8m (550ft x 65ft), with 7° ski ramp. Increased 1988 to 12°.
Deck Recognition Letter:	N
Pennant Number:	R05

Appendix Two
Commanding Officers HMS *Invincible*

Captain M. H. Livesay RN	1979-82
Captain J. J. Black MBE RN	1982-83
Captain The Hon N. J. Hill-Norton RN	1983-84
Captain C. H. Layman DSO MVO RN	1984-86
Captain M. P. Gretton RN	1988-90
Captain J. G. Tolhurst RN	1990-91
Captain F. M. Malbon RN	1991-93
Captain R. G. Hastilow RN	1993-95
Captain I. A. Forbes RN	1995-96
Captain R. A. G. Clare RN	1996-97
Captain J. M. Burnell-Nugent RN	1997-99
Captain R. A. I. McLean OBE RN	1999-2001
Captain T. A. Soar OBE RN	2002-04
Captain N. Morisetti BSc RN	2004-

Appendix Three

Former *Invincibles*

The First *Invincible* 1744-1758:

The first *Invincible* to serve with the Royal Navy was a 74-gun French ship, *l' Invincible,* which was captured off Finisterre in 1747. She was commissioned into the Royal Navy in 1748 and her advanced design provided a great deal of information to British naval architects. With a tonnage of 1,836, a length of 171 feet and a beam of 49 feet, *Invincible* had a crew of 700. In early 1758, commanded by Captain J. Bentley, she sailed with the expedition which captured Cape Breton Island. Unfortunately, soon after leaving harbour she ran aground on Dean Sand in the eastern approaches to Spithead and became a total loss.

The Second *Invincible* 1765-1801

The second *Invincible* was a 74-gun Third Rate, which was launched at Deptford in 1765. With a tonnage of 1,631, a length of 168 feet, a beam of 47 feet and a draught of 17 feet, she carried a complement of 600. On

29 December 1799 *Invincible* was part of Admiral Sir George Rodney's fleet of 22 ships of the line and nine frigates escorting a convoy for the besieged Crown Colony of Gibraltar, as well as trade with the West Indian islands, where Admiral Rodney was to take over command of the Leeward Islands Station. On 8 January 1800, Rodney's force intercepted six Spanish frigates and a merchant convoy of 16 ships bound for Cadiz and all the enemy ships were captured intact. Continuing south, some eight days later Rodney encountered another Spanish fleet comprising 11 ships of the line and two frigates which he chased and was able to engage. The battle continued into the night and British superiority soon began to tell. By dawn six Spanish ships had been taken and *Invincible* had won her first battle honour. In September 1781 *Invincible* was part of a fleet of 27 ships which fought an action with the French off the Chesapeake towards the end of the American War of Independence. Due to indecision and lack of resolution the British fleet retired to New York to

The Audacious-class, central-battery ironclad HMS *Invincible* which was launched in May 1869. She ended her days in Portsmouth as part of the apprentices' training establishment HMS *Fisgard:* she was lost off Portland in September 1914.

(Adrian Vicary, Maritime Photo Library)

refit, leaving the French in possession of Chesapeake Bay and the way clear for Cornwallis's defeat and surrender a few weeks later. In January 1782 *Invincible* was one of 30 ships commanded by Admiral Hood which put to sea to engage a French fleet which was thought to be close to the island of St Kitts. On 25 January the fleets met and following a furious action the French withdrew, leaving Hood in possession of the roadstead. A year later, in February 1783, *Invincible* closed and recaptured the frigate *Argo,* which had been taken three days earlier, from the French.

Invincible's third battle honour, the 'Glorious First of June', marked the battle in the North Atlantic between Admiral Lord Howe and the French Admiral Villaret-Joyeuse, which was the first major encounter at sea between the warring countries. Apart from a chart reference the battle had no geographical location and the outcome was not clear-cut, although on the face of it Howe triumphed which is reflected in the name given to the battle. After three weeks of patient patrolling in the Western Approaches by Howe's 34 ships of the line, on 28 May 1794 his flagship *Queen Charlotte* sighted the French fleet of 26 ships of the line. For three days the French fleet resisted Howe's attempts to reach a large French merchant convoy to the south, but on 1 June, a clear, fine day, the opposing fleets were just four miles apart. Having gained the windward position Howe bore down on the French line intending to break through at all points and destroy the enemy fleet. Unfortunately, due to misunderstandings most of the fleet failed to break through and the result was a general mêlée. Six French of the line struck their colours and two foundered, but the remainder escaped. During the action *Invincible* was badly damaged, with her fore, main and top masts shot away. She suffered 14 killed and 31 wounded.

In February 1797 *Invincible* was part of the fleet which captured Trinidad and bombarded San Juan on the island of Puerto Rico. Two years later, in August 1799, she assisted in the capture of the Dutch island of Surinam. On 16 March 1801, flying the flag of Rear-Admiral Totty and commanded by Captain J. Rennie RN, *Invincible* left Nelson's fleet off Copenhagen to return to Portsmouth. Whilst *Invincible* was sailing off the Norfolk coast and course had been set through the deep water channel dividing two sandbanks through what is known as the 'Haseborough Gateway', just out of sight of the tall tower of Happisburgh Church, a familiar landmark to mariners, she ran off course and grounded. Heavily laden with ordnance and stores she was stuck fast, but her captain was confident she could be refloated on the next tide. As a precaution her boats were lowered and efforts were made to lighten her as much as possible, with the yards and top masts being cut down and stores being thrown overboard, but not before a fierce storm blew up which not only swept

away the boats but also began to break up the ship. On the following day she slid off the shoal and sank in deep water with the loss of 400 lives, including Captain Rennie. The injured were taken to hospital at Great Yarmouth where they were visited by Horatio Nelson, and some 119 of those who lost their lives were buried in an unmarked mass grave at the north-east end of St Mary's Church, Happisburgh. It was in 1997 that this was revealed, and *Invincible's* ship's company co-operated with local people to erect a memorial on the mound which was said to conceal their remains.

The Third *Invincible* 1808-1861

Launched at Woolwich in 1808 the third *Invincible* was another 74-gun Third Rate, with a length of 170 feet, a beam of 48 feet and a draught of 18 feet. During the Napoleonic Wars she assisted Spanish patriots in the defence of Cadiz and Tarragona against the French, and in 1813 she captured two French privateers at Ampolla. In 1814 she assisted with the reduction of Fort St Philip near Barcelona. *Invincible's* final years were spent as an ammunition depot ship, and later as a coal depot ship at Devonport. She was broken up in 1861.

The Fourth *Invincible* 1869-1904

Built at the Govan shipyard of R. Napier, the fourth *Invincible* was an Audacious-class, central-battery ironclad, which was launched on 29 May 1869. Completed 17 months later, she had a tonnage of 6,010, a length of 280 feet and a beam of 54 feet. Armed with ten 9-inch and four 6-inch muzzle-loading guns, she was powered by steam reciprocating engines which gave her a speed of 14 knots, and she carried a complement of 450. In July 1882, during the Egyptian War, *Invincible* formed part of Admiral Sir Frederick Beauchamp Seymour's fleet which bombarded the defensive forts around the city of Alexandria. She also contributed a Naval Brigade which took part in the land campaign. Between 1880 and 1890 she was guard ship at Southampton and in 1901 a destroyer depot ship at Sheerness. In 1904, when the new battlecruiser *Invincible* was laid down, she was renamed *Erebus* and for a time she was placed on the sale list. However, when it became necessary to enlarge the boy artificers' training establishment at Portsmouth, she was fitted up with machinery for instructional purposes and she became part of HMS *Fisgard II*. In the autumn of 1914 it was decided to move her to Devonport, but on 16 September 1914 just a few weeks after the outbreak of war, whilst under tow and with only a navigating crew on board, she foundered in gale force winds five miles off Portland Bill. Although a passing merchantman responded to her distress signals, the high winds and heavy seas impeded the rescue work and 21 men were drowned. At the time, with the great European powers tearing themselves to pieces on the battlefields of

The ill-fated battlecruiser *Invincible* seen here in 1912, two years before the outbreak of the First World War.
(Adrian Vicary, Maritime Photo Library)

Belching black smoke, *Invincible* is seen here at speed on 8 December 1914, during the Battle of the Falkland Islands.
(Adrian Vicary, Maritime Photo Library)

France and the lists of casualties taking up ever more space in the newspapers of the day, there was little interest in the fate of an elderly Victorian warship.

The Fifth *Invincible* 1907-1916

Launched on 13 April 1907 by Lady Alexandrina Allendale, at the Elswick shipyard of Sir W. G. Armstrong Whitworth & Co on the River Tyne, the fifth *Invincible* gave her name to a class of three 17,200-ton battlecruisers. Built to carry big guns on lightly armoured hulls, the battlecruisers were designed with speed in mind, but they were controversial ships which could not match battleships punch for punch. With a length of 530 feet, a beam of 78 feet and a draught of 26 feet, *Invincible's* main armament consisted of eight 12-inch guns and she was powered by Parsons steam turbines, which drove her four propellers and gave her a speed of 26 knots. Her design resembled that of an armoured cruiser rather than a capital ship, and she was the first British warship to be fitted with all-electric

machinery for working her 12-inch gun turrets. This was not a success, however, and it was removed in March 1914 and replaced with hydraulic machinery.

On 28 August 1914, within weeks of the outbreak of war, *Invincible* was involved in the Battle of Heligoland Bight, and in December the same year, flying the flag of Vice-Admiral Sir Doveton Sturdee, she took part in the Battle of the Falkland Islands. Together with her sister *Inflexible* and five cruisers, she sank two German armoured cruisers and two light cruisers, thereby avenging the Royal Navy's defeat at Coronel.

On 31 May 1916, at Jutland, *Invincible* was the flagship of Rear-Admiral H. L. A. Hood's Third Battlecruiser Squadron. At 18.00 that day, some 60 miles west of the Jutland peninsula, she fell victim to the devastatingly accurate gunnery of *Derflinger* and *Lutzow* and she blew up. Of her wartime complement of 1,034 there were only six survivors.

Appendix Four

Battle Honours

HMS *Invincible*

St Vincent 1780	Heligoland 1914
St Kitts 1782	Falkland Islands 1914
Glorious First of June 1794	Jutland 1916
Alexandria 1882	Falkland Islands 1982

Acknowledgements

My thanks to Rear-Admiral R. A. G. Clare, Director National Maritime Museum for kindly contributing the Foreword to this book, also to Rear-Admiral Trevor Soar OBE Royal Navy; Commander David Elford, Royal Navy; Lieutenant Mark Warrick, Royal Navy; Petty Officer (Phot) Paul Smith; MEMAPP Ian Spanner and the ship's company of HMS *Invincible* (October 2003) for their kind help and hospitality.

My thanks also to: - Roger Beacham and the staff of Cheltenham Reference Library: Michael Cassar, Valletta, Malta: Leslie Cheyne, Sedgefield, Co Durham: Dave Cullen, Edinburgh: Lyn Dunning, Arts & Museums Service, Town Hall, Barrow-in-Furness, Cumbria: Derek Fox, Southsea, Hampshire: Ross Gillett OAM, Senior Public Relations Officer, Royal Australian Navy, (New South Wales): James Goss, Southsea, Hampshire: Sara Hadwin, Editor, Furness Newspapers, Barrow-in-Furness, Cumbria: Brian Hargreaves, Tynemouth: Vic Jeffery OAM, Senior Public Relations Officer, Royal Australian Navy (Western Australia): Mike Lennon, Waterlooville, Hampshire: David Lippman, Portsmouth, Hampshire: A. J. (Tony) Perrett, Gosport, Hampshire: Drew Rance, Babcock Engineering Services, Rosyth: Walter Sartori, Portsmouth, Hampshire: Jerry Shore, Assistant Curator, Fleet Air Arm Museum, RNAS Yeovilton, Somerset: Don Smith, Selby, Nth Yorkshire: Mike Smith, BAE SYSTEMS, Barrow-in-Furness, Cumbria: Alan Sparrow, Billingham, Cleveland: Ian Spashett, Folkestone, Kent: Derek Taylor, Colchester, Essex: Adrian Vicary, Maritime Photo Library, Cromer, Norfolk: Steve Wiseman, Westbury-on-Trym, Bristol: Staff of the National Archives (formerly Public Record Office), Kew, Surrey: Finally, to my wife Freda and my daughter Louise for all their help and support.

Other Titles Available

HMS *Eagle* 1942-1978 £18.95

Three *Ark Royals* 1938-1999 £23

Tiger, Lion and Blake 1942-1986 £21.50

The Illustrious and Implacable Classes of Aircraft Carrier 1940-1969 £23

HMS *Hermes* 1923 & 1959 £24

The Colossus-Class Aircraft Carriers 1944-1972 £24

HMS *Vanguard* 1944-1960 £19.95

HMS *Glory* 1945-1961 £19.95

Fearless & Intrepid 1965-2002 £24

SS *Canberra* 1957-1997 £21

(Plus £2.75 postage in the UK/EU or £4.50 worldwide surface mail)

FAN PUBLICATIONS
17 Wymans Lane
Cheltenham
Glos GL51 9QA
Tel/Fax: 01242 580290
E-mail: info@fan-publications.i12.com